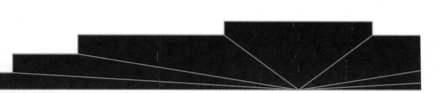

INTRODUCTION

LIVERPOOL HAD TO WAIT A LONG TIME TO WITNESS THE SPECTACULAR ARRIVAL OF A CUNARD QUEEN IN THE MERSEY.

That day came in July 1990 as the most famous name in passenger shipping celebrated the 150th anniversary of its founding and the departure of its first scheduled transatlantic service from Liverpool to North America.

In the intervening 21 years, Queen Elizabeth 2 returned to Cunard Line's spiritual home a further eight times.

Her mighty sister, Queen Mary 2, has called once, and the luxurious liner Queen Victoria has made her maiden call too. Each of these visits has created a new chapter in the city's rich maritime history.

The appearance of the brick-red livery of the Cunard funnel on the Mersey stirs memories among many associated with the line and the city.

These visits serve to fire the imagination of tens of thousands of spectators with no previous connection with either the port or Cunard Line – spectators who flock to the banks of the Mersey to witness the majestic arrivals and spectacular departures of these great ocean liners.

Now it is the turn of the newest Cunarder – Queen Elizabeth – to follow in the wake of her illustrious sisters, cross the Mersey Bar and head gracefully up the Mersey to her berth at Pier Head, just a stone's throw away from the famous Cunard Building.

It promises to be another memorable day. So too, a week later, will be the return to Liverpool of the Line's flagship Queen Mary 2.

Each of these visits is sure to reaffirm the historic 171-year old link between Liverpool and Cunard Line. The River Mersey is once again set to welcome the Cunard Queens – the most famous ocean liners in the world.

TONY STOREY,
AUTHOR & EDITOR, CUNARD QUEENS OF THE MERSEY

CUNARD

QUEENS OF THE MERSEY

QUEEN ELIZABETH + QUEEN MARY 2
AN HISTORIC HOMECOMING

Published by:
Trinity Mirror Media
PO Box 48, Old Hall Street, Liverpool L69 3EB

Business Development Director:
Mark Dickinson

Executive Editor:
Ken Rogers

Cunard Queens of the Mersey Editor:
Tony Storey

Design / Production:
Colin Harrison

Additional Design / Production:
Vicky Andrews, Rick Cooke, Paul Dove

Written by:
Tony Storey

Trinity Mirror Media

© Pictures and text, unless otherwise stated:
Trinity Mirror / Liverpool Daily Post & Echo / Cunard Archive /
Cruise Media Services

The publishers are grateful to the following individuals
and organisations for the assistance given in producing this
commemorative publication: Peter Shanks;
Eric Flounders; Michael Gallagher (Cunard Line);
Jacqueline Hodgson, Hotel Manager, Queen Elizabeth;
Anthony Inglis (www.anthonyinglis.com)
and Fincantieri Cantieri Navali Italiani S.p.A.

Printed by Pensord
ISBN 978-1-906802-59-2

FOREWORD

CUNARD
THE MOST FAMOUS OCEAN LINERS IN THE WORLD ™

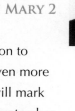

IT MUST BE CLOSE TO HALF A CENTURY SINCE TWO CUNARDERS HAVE BEEN SEEN ON THE MERSEY WITHIN THE SPACE OF SEVEN DAYS, BUT THAT WILL BE THE MARVELLOUS SPECTACLE IN SEPTEMBER 2011 WHEN QUEEN ELIZABETH MAKES HER MAIDEN CALL FOLLOWED BY OUR FLAGSHIP QUEEN MARY 2 MAKING HER SECOND CALL JUST SEVEN DAYS LATER.

As always a visit by a Cunard ship to our spiritual home is a reason to celebrate and we intend to do just that! The celebrations will be even more prominent this year as Queen Elizabeth's arrival on 8 September will mark the start of River Festival Week. Queen Mary 2's departure on 15 September will conclude the week-long festival.

The third Cunarder to bear the name 'Elizabeth', our new Queen entered service last year and is a beautiful, gracious and modern ocean liner with wonderful warm art deco touches right around the ship. A sister to the warmly received Queen Victoria, she has her own distinct personality that pays tribute to the Elizabeths that have gone before her with memorabilia and reminders of those very special ships.

We were both honoured and proud that Her Majesty The Queen named our new liner in Southampton on Monday, 11 October 2010. The naming was a milestone in British maritime history and was a major event of worldwide interest. Her Majesty was present at the age of 12 at the launch of the first Queen Elizabeth on 27 September 1938 when she accompanied her mother, Queen Elizabeth, to Clydebank for the launch. And Her Majesty launched QE2 on 20 September 1967. Queen Elizabeth, the second largest Cunarder ever built, will take this historic name far into the 21st Century.

Queen Mary 2 is the flagship of the most famous brand at sea – one of the oldest names in shipping with the youngest fleet afloat – and her second visit to Liverpool is sure to be as exciting as the first.

This magnificent liner, a splendid heir to the great Cunard liners and tradition that has gone before her, is still the largest passenger ship ever to sail up the Mersey and what a sight she will make tied up along the Liverpool Cruise Facility within sight of the magnificent Cunard Building on the Pier Head. Liverpool – here we come!

PETER SHANKS
PRESIDENT & MANAGING DIRECTOR, CUNARD LINE

CONTENTS

An Enduring Union Between Cunard Line and Liverpool

Samual Cunard. Above, the paddle steamer Britannia

CUNARD LINE'S NEWEST LUXURY LINER QUEEN ELIZABETH WILL ARRIVE ON HER MAIDEN MERSEY CALL ON 8 SEPTEMBER, MARKING A WEEK OF MARITIME CELEBRATIONS IN THE CITY THAT SAW THE CREATION OF THE MOST FAMOUS SHIPPING LINE IN THE WORLD.

Seven days later the Line's mighty flagship Queen Mary 2 will make its second call at Liverpool – with each historic visit set to reaffirm the strong links between the city and Cunard.

The new Cunarder will reach Liverpool just a little more than 171 years after the first ship to bear the great founder's name left the port bound for Nova Scotia.

Samuel Cunard himself was on board the paddle steamer Britannia as she pulled away from Coburg Dock to start his line's maiden crossing of the North Atlantic. The vessel, small enough

to fit inside a restaurant on board Queen Mary 2, made the crossing in a fortnight. The voyage marked a revolution in the means of communication of the day. This was, after all, a time when mail and newspapers could take weeks to reach parts of the world.

Having proved the relative speed and efficiency of his North Atlantic service, Cunard secured a valuable contract with the Admiralty to run mail on a weekly service sailing every Saturday from Liverpool to either Halifax or Boston.

By this time the pioneering engineering in Britannia had been carried across to a fleet of sister ships. Between them, these vessels set the course on which Cunard Line has criss-crossed the oceans of the world ever since.

Cunard's first ships were far removed from the luxury associated with them now; indeed, Cunard and luxury were total strangers. Like the man, the ships were plain and practical.

Cabins were small, each divided from the next by a mere partition.

Top: Britannia stuck in the ice in Boston Harbour in 1844

Passengers were responsible for washing their own plates and cutlery, though eating was often far from their minds in inclement weather as they paddled about below decks ankle deep in water. "There's water pouring down the stairs," exclaimed one early passenger to an officer. "We only worry, madam", he replied "when it's coming up the stairs".

Fresh meat ran out early in each voyage, after which salted was all that was available, and milk was supplied by a hapless cow slung on the deck in a hammock.

But uncomfortable and basic though they were, Cunard's steamships had two great advantages over sailing ships: firstly, they got the agony over more quickly – 10 days as opposed to six weeks – and secondly they were steadfastly safe and reliable.

Samuel Cunard himself made safety his priority – and to this day Cunard has never been responsible for the loss of a single passenger or a single mailbag on the Atlantic run.

Cunard's original instruction to his first master, Captain Woodroffe, was simply: "Speed is nothing…safety is all that is required" and that has been followed religiously by the company ever since.

Departure of a Cunard steamer from Liverpool; London News, 1881

DEPARTURE OF A CUNARD STEAM-SHIP FROM LIVERPOOL.

Cunard's safety record – which was such that passengers would refuse to board other Line's ships but insist on waiting for the next Cunarder – together with the mail contract, made Cunard profits.

But the company's first excursion into war produced a serious risk to that prosperity. In 1854, 14 Cunard ships – almost the entire fleet – were requisitioned for the Crimean War.

While the company's contribution to the war effort was remarkable – including transporting all the horses that charged with the Light Brigade – all Cunard mail services on the Atlantic stopped, and competition, notably the much-subsidised American Collins Line, won Cunard's lucrative business by default. Crimea gave Samuel Cunard a baronetcy – but it gave Collins a virtual monopoly on the Atlantic.

However, over-expansion and a cavalier attitude to safety did for Collins, which, despite being subsidised by the American government at twice the value of Cunard's mail contract provided 'its ships could outstrip Cunard', went bankrupt in 1858. Cunard regained its pre-eminence.

Cunard vessels transported horses for the army during the Crimea War. Cornet Henry Wilkin, 11th Hussars, British Army during the Crimea War. Photo by Roger Fenton (a pioneering British photographer and one of the first war photographers)

Cunard Liner The China on her maiden voyage in 1862

Carpathia, maiden voyage in 1903

Samuel Cunard's innate conservatism, which made the founding of the company so remarkable, flared up again in the late 1850s when he steadfastly refused to contemplate the change from paddle wheels to propellers – despite mounting evidence that screw propulsion was more efficient, more powerful and released more space.

He only relented in 1862 with the construction of The China – after first having to seek the permission of the Admiralty as the mail contract specified paddle steamers.

But the China also hinted at a coming decline in the importance of the mail contract, as it was the first ship specifically to cater for emigrants. And so emigration became Cunard's next guarantee of prosperity. Between 1860 and 1900, 14 million people emigrated from Europe to the United States; of those, 9 million passed through Liverpool with a sizeable proportion of the immense total making the voyage to America with Cunard.

Cunard's next challenge was the introduction of a floating hotel, spearheaded by the newly-formed White Star's Oceanic in 1870.

Where Oceanic had bathtubs, Cunard offered a basin; where Oceanic had central heating, Cunard offered stoves; where Oceanic had taps, Cunard offered jugs; where Oceanic had lamps, Cunard offered candles; and where Oceanic had lavatories, Cunard managed with chamber pots.

Declining revenues forced Cunard to follow suit, and even to innovate. The Servia of 1881 was the first steel Cunarder, the first to be built with an electricity supply, the first to have ensuite bathrooms and the first

budgeted to rely solely on passenger revenue. The reliance on the mail diminished even more.

1902 saw the virtually unnoticed launch on the Tyne of a minor Cunarder destined for the Mediterranean trade – and also destined to become one of the most famous ships of all time.

She was the 13,600-ton Carpathia which, in 1912, achieved immortality under the command of Captain Arthur Rostron when she sped through ice fields in the night, without the benefit of modern radar and at a speed greater than she was supposedly capably of, to rescue all the survivors of the Titanic. The plucky Carpathia will be remembered during the 2012 commemoration of the 100th anniversary of the loss of Titanic.

Captain Rostron, later Commodore of the Cunard fleet, master of the Queen Mary, and knighted by the King, remarked later that a hand greater than his own guided the little ship that night.

But that was glory yet to come; at the same time as Carpathia was entering service Cunard was looking none too glorious, battered as the company's ageing transatlantic fleet was by ferocious competition from the Germans and Americans.

However, Cunard's fight back led to the introduction of three of the company's most famous ships – Lusitania, Mauretania and Aquitania.

A scene from the documentary Lusitania: Murder on the Atlantic

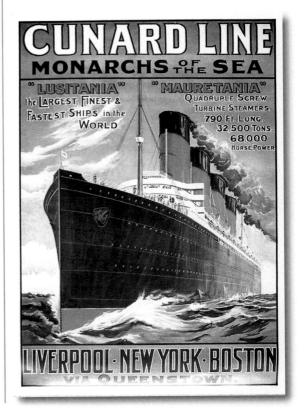

The view from Seacombe promenade in July 1913 with ships dressed overall in mid-river. Cunard's four-funnelled Mauretania can be seen far right

These were the first 'floating palaces' in the Cunard fleet – palaces which moved at unprecedented speed. The Mauretania held the Blue Riband record for Transatlantic crossings for 22 years.

Again the company was drawn into conflict when its ships were requisitioned for the First World War.

During the four years of carnage, Cunard ships transported over a million men, served as hospital ships, prisoner-of-war ships, food and munitions carriers, and as armed merchant cruisers. It was in the latter role that the Carmania had the distinction of taking the first German casualty of the war when she sank the Cap Trafalgar – ironically disguised as Carmania – off South America in November 1914.

Campania, meanwhile, was equipped with a 240-foot long platform and so became the forerunner of today's aircraft carriers.

All in all, over 22 Cunard ships were lost – including the unrequisitioned Lusitania, torpedoed by U20 off the Old Head of Kinsale in 1915 with the loss of 1,200 civilian lives.

The interwar years, bolstered by the addition to the fleet as part of war reparations the former German vessel Imperator, renamed Berengaria, were successful and lucrative for Cunard – so much so that the company failed to notice the significance of Charles Lindbergh's transatlantic flight in 1927.

Nonetheless, the first real move from reliance on transatlantic revenues was made when, in 1921, Laconia undertook the first-ever World Cruise.

Cunard did not set out to create in 1928 what King George V called "the stateliest ship now in being", and nor did it intend to give birth to a ship which her last Master, Captain John Treasure Jones, said was "the nearest ship ever to be a living being".

It was purely by circumstance that the company produced a ship which more graphically shared the country's triumphs and tribulations, and which was more loved by people who had never even seen her, let alone set foot on her, than any which had gone before.

Cunard's intention in 1928 had been simply to replace its ageing transatlantic fleet with a new pair of steamships, which could provide a weekly service in each direction and so meet the growing challenge of German competition on the North Atlantic.

When the first of the pair, Number 534, later to be named Queen Mary, was revealed to be the largest and most powerful ship ever built, the Chairman of Cunard, Sir Percy Bates, diffidently said she was just "the smallest and slowest ship which could accomplish such a service".

Work on Number 534 began at the Clydebank yard of John Brown and Co late in 1930. She was being built at an estimated cost of £6.5 million out of Cunard revenue, without the benefit of any state subsidy.

Almost alone at the time Cunard operated on the North Atlantic as a commercial concern; every other major line was subsidised to a significant degree by its national government, but Cunard was expected not only to compete but to ensure Britain remained dominant on the North Atlantic without a penny of state aid.

The company did so until the Depression cut revenues of £9 million in 1928 to under £4 million in 1931, and despite Cunard staff on shore and at sea taking a pay cut, work on the construction of Queen Mary stopped just before Christmas 1931.

Queen Mary in Sydney Harbour Austraila

Immediately 3,640 men in Clydebank – a town where half the wages came from Queen Mary – were thrown out of work. But the ripples were felt by 10,000 ancillary workers further away. They were felt in Stoke-on-Trent, busy working on 200,000 pieces of crockery; in Sheffield, where 100,000 items of cutlery were being crafted; in Walsall, which was producing 400 tons of tubes; in Rugby, manufacturing seven turbo-generators; in Liverpool, producing 2,500 square feet of toughened glass; in Millwall, casting four 20-foot propellers; in Darlington, forging the 190-ton stern frame; in Belfast, working on the 5.5 ton gear wheels; in Halifax, weaving 10 miles of blankets; in St Albans, producing 600 clocks; and in other towns up and down the land making curtains, carpets, anchor chains and furniture. All of them stopped.

The rusting skeleton of Queen Mary, with 80 per cent of the hull rivets in place and £1.5 million already spent, was symbolic of the financial catastrophe which hit both Britain and America.

It was such a graphic symbol of which the general population was so conscious, that members of the public sent thousands of unsolicited donations of money to Cunard in an effort to get the work restarted.

The Government was implored to lend Cunard the capital to complete the ship and get so many back to work – but the Government unswervingly refused – until 1934, that is, when, in a complex deal which required Cunard to take over the running of White Star's ailing transatlantic fleet, Neville Chamberlain, then the Chancellor of the Exchequer, agreed to lend Cunard sufficient funds to complete Queen Mary and build her sister, Queen Elizabeth.

And so, on 3 April 1934, the John Brown workforce, led by a Pipe Band, returned to work and began by removing 130 tons of rust and dozens of nesting crows.

Just five months later Queen Mary, wife of King George V, became the first monarch to launch a merchant ship, a job which she accomplished with a bottle of Australian wine rather than the traditional French champagne.

As she said the words, broadcast over the radio, "I name this ship Queen Mary; may God bless her and all who sail in her" millions of the King's subjects heard his wife's voice for the very first time.

Two hundred thousand spectators watched the launch – and many, on the opposite bank of the Clyde, got wet as an eight foot wave surged across the river when the enormous hull entered the water.

A popular story has it that Cunard's Board had not intended to name the ship Queen Mary, and, to stick to the traditional 'ia' endings prevalent among the Cunard transatlantic fleet, they despatched one of their members, Lord Royden, to ask his friend the King for permission to name the ship 'Queen Victoria'.

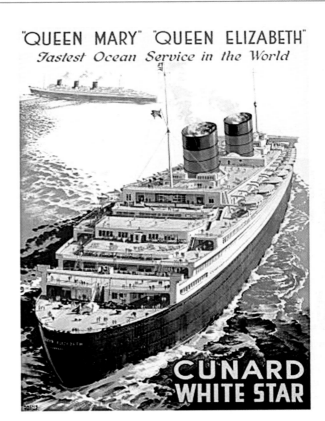

"QUEEN MARY" "QUEEN ELIZABETH"
Fastest Ocean Service in the World

CUNARD WHITE STAR

Queen Mary
leaving NewYork

The Queen Mother,
then the Duchess
of York, after the
christening of Princess
Elizabeth. Behind her is
the then Duke of York
with Queen Mary and
King George V

Allegedly, he didn't ask directly but intimated that Cunard would like to name the ship after "England's most illustrious Queen". "My wife will be delighted", replied King George, "I will go and tell her now".

A good story – but not true. Cunard had already decided that since the White Star and Cunard transatlantic fleets had been combined under the new banner Cunard White Star, neither the traditional White Star 'ic' ending nor the Cunard 'ia' ending was appropriate. The first ship of the new company needed to break with tradition – and Queen Mary it was intended to be.

The maiden voyage began in Southampton on 27 May 1936, and Queen Mary left to the sounds of bands and ecstatic crowds. On board were the famous bandleader, Henry Hall, scheduled to give a series of live radio broadcasts during the crossing; the virtuoso harmonica player, Larry Adler; and a well-known singer of the time, Frances Day, who performed a song written specially for Queen Mary by Henry Hall, 'Somewhere at Sea'. And, much as she may have liked being at sea, Miss Day did not trust the ship's eggs to be fresh by the end of the voyage so she took along her own hens.

The rapturous welcome in New York on 1 June 1936 marked the completion of the first voyage of four years of glamorous transatlantic service, during which Queen Mary gained the Blue Riband twice for the fastest Atlantic crossing.

The sister ship to Queen Mary – Queen Elizabeth – had a less glorious start. She was launched in 1938 by Queen Elizabeth, wife of George VI – who could not be present himself because the growing pressures of impending war kept him in London – accompanied by Princess Elizabeth, the present Queen, and Princess Margaret.

As fitting-out work was progressing it was decided that not only was Queen Elizabeth a target for German air attacks, but she was also occupying Clydeside shipyard space required for the war effort. She had to move.

The Captain put to sea, with workmen still on board, and once out of the Clyde opened his sealed orders which he expected to instruct him to go to Southampton; instead, he was told to head at full speed to New York. The secret dash was done with the launching gear still affixed to the underside of the ship, and without proper fitments inside.

Men who expected to be going home by trains from Southampton within days did not get home for years.

After trooping from Australia, Queen Mary and Queen Elizabeth began bringing American GIs across to Europe in 1942 at full speed and unescorted. Not only were they faster than the U-Boats whose crews had been offered £100,000 by Hitler to sink either of them, but they were faster even than the torpedoes. In summer, 15,000 soldiers were carried on each voyage – such a huge number that the men had to sleep in shifts, observing a strict one-way system on board.

Queen Mary's master, Commodore Sir James Bisset, noted that the ship was so difficult to handle under such circumstances that he was concerned for her stability. All told, she made 28 such trips, taking soldiers eastbound and prisoners-of-war westbound, with Queen Elizabeth undertaking a similar number. On three occasions Queen Mary was the nerve-centre of the Empire as Sir Winston Churchill crossed the Atlantic to see President Roosevelt.

The trooping record of the two Queens, together with Aquitania, reduced the duration of the war – according to Churchill – by at least a year.

After the war Queen Mary and Queen Elizabeth had a golden period, doing what they were built to do. This was the era of film stars and royalty being photographed by hundreds of press photographers as they stepped ashore in Southampton or New York. But in 1958 the ghost of that Lindbergh flight caught up with Cunard, as for the first time, more people crossed the Atlantic by air than by sea. The end was in sight.

The Queen Mother, then Queen Elizabeth, and King George VI during a war time visit to Liverpool

Below Left: Queen Elizabeth on an early voyage

Below: Embarking Australian troops on to Queen May during World War 2

Queen Mary in a Clydeside dock with her port of registry emblazoned on her stern

Finally, she left New York for the last time on 22 September 1967 – her 1,001st voyage. This was just two days after the launch by Her Majesty The Queen of Queen Elizabeth 2. During the crossing she passed Queen Elizabeth for the last time, just a mile distant, at a combined speed of 60 knots.

Having carried 2,114,000 passengers, plus 810,730 military personnel, 19,000 GI brides and 4,000 child evacuees, and having travelled 3,794,017 nautical miles, Queen Mary left on her last journey from Southampton on 31 October 1967, bound for her present home in Long Beach California. On board were two double-decker London buses, and the passengers on board delighted in rounding Cape Horn on a bus.

She arrived to an ecstatic welcome in Long Beach where she remains today – officially now a building, rather than one of the greatest ships ever built.

Queen Elizabeth ended her career just a year later in an ignominious fashion, just as she had

started it in less triumphant circumstances than Queen Mary. Sold by Cunard in 1968, she eventually ended up in Hong Kong to undergo conversion into a floating university. There, in 1972, a number of mysterious fires broke out simultaneously and, inundated by millions of gallons of water from fire hoses, the ship turned over and sank – her side visible above the water.

The sale of Queen Mary and Queen Elizabeth was the nadir in Cunard's fortunes. Towards the end the ships had been criss-crossing the Atlantic virtually empty – on one voyage Queen Elizabeth had only 200 passengers – and in so doing they were losing the company £4 million a year each.

And yet, in the face of all evidence to the contrary and in what seemed to many an act of lunacy equal only to Samuel Cunard's original madness in establishing the company, the Cunard board – as it pensioned off two transatlantic liners which had been defeated by the jet aircraft – was planning to construct another transatlantic liner.

And so Queen Elizabeth 2, a true transatlantic liner with a service speed of 28.5 knots and a 1.5 inch thick hull, but which, with its ability to navigate both Panama and Suez, could be a cruise ship too, was launched by the Queen in 1967.

She was already famous when she slid down the slipway as a result of intense press speculation about her name, secret to the last. (Sir Winston Churchill and Princess Anne had been among the bookie's favourites). And from that point she has never been out of public scrutiny, and she remains the most famous ship in the world.

QE2 – as she rapidly became – did not have an auspicious start. Her Keel Laying in 1965 was delayed by three days as the crane destined to place the keel in place toppled over instead.

On her sea trials in 1968 recurring turbine problems were followed by a total breakdown off the Canaries, as a result of which QE2 limped into her homeport on her first call at Southampton in January 1969. Cunard refused to accept delivery, six advertised cruises were cancelled – and the Maiden Voyage had to be delayed until May.

As if this did not bring gloom enough, city analysts predicted QE2 would never make a profit, and would be mothballed within six months – the last fling of a defunct company, a white elephant.

The most famous ship in the world sold serenely on for 41 years calling at Liverpool nine times to maintain the great tradition started in 1840.

And what a dramatic 41 years they were.

Queen Elizabeth 2 during construction on the Clyde

Flagship of the British Merchant Fleet in the South Atlantic war zone

In 1972, a threat was made by an American extortionist to blow up QE2 in mid-Atlantic by means of suicide accomplices on board, unless a ransom was paid.

Although the ship already had comprehensive search routines in place, as a precaution Cunard arranged with the Ministry of Defence for SAS personnel to be parachuted into the sea near to QE2. A further search was carried out, but no explosives were found. However the extortionist was caught and ended up in prison on a 20-year sentence.

Just a year later, according to the former President of Egypt, Anwar Sadat, Colonel Gadaffi planned to torpedo QE2 as she passed through the Mediterranean – and only Sadat's last-minute intervention prevented the attack.

In 1976 three members of the IRA were arrested trying to take explosives on board QE2.

On 4 May 1982, en route to Southampton from Philadelphia, Queen Elizabeth 2 was requisitioned by the Government for service in the Falklands Campaign and so joined the ranks of the great Cunarders called upon to serve their country.

Conversion work to prepare the ship for trooping duties began the following day.

Helicopter landing pads were constructed

on the Quarter Deck forward from the Bridge and aft over the two swimming pools – the former possibly constituting, when the ship was travelling at speed, one of the most hazardous landing areas any pilot could wish to encounter.

Valuable paintings and furniture were removed, piping for refuelling at sea laid through passenger areas, and hardboard placed over carpets.

Equipment, rations, vehicles, fuel and spare parts were loaded aboard – so much that a great deal had to be stored on the open deck.

To man the ship, Cunard asked for volunteers from among its employees to go to the war zone; it required 650, and it got over 1,000.

Left: A Sea King helicopter lands on board the QE2 during the Falklands Campaign

On 12 May, 3,000 men of the Fifth Infantry Brigade comprising units of the Scots Guards, the Welsh Guards and the Gurkha Rifles, along with naval personnel, came aboard and QE2, under the command of Captain Peter Jackson, put to sea and headed south.

On the journey southwards from Freetown, the only port of call, every one of the liner's portholes was covered with black plastic to provide a total blackout: from being the ocean's brightest star, QE2 – for her own safety – became the darkest.

On 22 May news came through of the loss of the Atlantic Conveyor, a Cunard ship also serving in the Falklands Campaign. This was a particularly bleak day as many of the QE2's crew had friends aboard the Atlantic Conveyor; the news of heavy loss of life caused enormous sadness.

On the last leg of the outbound voyage, on 23 May, the navigation lights were extinguished and the radar turned off in order to silence the ship electronically.

This deprived QE2's navigating officers of a vital aid, and put them back almost half a century. But the situation became particularly grave once the ship entered icefields north of South Georgia. Huge icebergs were encountered on the night of 26 May – many bigger than the ship – and to compound a serious situation, fog reduced visibility to less than a mile.

On 27 May, QE2 anchored in Cumberland Bay, South Georgia, where the tricky job of transferring troops and supplies to other vessels began. In total darkness, requisitioned trawlers carried out the enormously difficult task of shuttling between the blacked-out vessels.

The transfer of troops and stores was completed on 29 May, after which 640 survivors of HMS Ardent, Coventry and Antelope came aboard for the journey back to Ascension Island.

Shortly before the scheduled day of arrival at Ascension on 4 June, orders were received from the Ministry of Defence that QE2 was to proceed instead to Southampton with the survivors.

At 0900 hours on 11 June, QE2 passed the Needles. Two hours later the survivors of Ardent, Coventry and Antelope mustered on deck to be greeted by Her Majesty Queen Elizabeth the Queen Mother, waving from the Britannia. As a further gesture, the Queen Mother radioed a message of welcome to QE2.

So finally, 12.5 days after leaving South Georgia, and almost 15,000 miles since first setting out from Southampton over a month earlier, Queen Elizabeth 2 was home, having done what was required of her in the service of the country.

QE2 arrives home from South Atlantic service

But not all the highlights of QE2's career have been so dramatic.

In 1990, during her first call at Liverpool, over one million people turned out to welcome her. Later in the same week, the Queen boarded in Southampton – her first visit since the ship's introduction to service.

In 1983, conscious of QE2's pulling power, Cunard decided to invest £110 million in replacing the 20-year old steam turbine engines with diesel electric engines.

On 20 October 1986, QE2 left New York for her last ever crossing as a steamship: QE2's last and Cunard's last. Cunard had been the first company to offer a timetabled steamship service across the Atlantic, and, despite war, depression and foreign competition, it was now the last to do so. But QE2 re-emerged the following year to carry on that tradition – with a new propulsion system and a renewed life expectancy.

It was generally thought at that point that QE2 would be the last ever transatlantic liner. When she's gone, everybody said, there will never be another.

People were about to be proved wrong again.

One of the first things announced by Carnival Corporation when they purchased Cunard in 1998 was the construction of a new transatlantic liner to follow in the glorious wake of Britannia, Mauretania, Aquitania, Queen Mary, Queen Elizabeth and QE2.

A heritage everyone thought was bound to die lives on – together with Cunard Line's unique connection to Liverpool.

Cunard Line's flagship Queen Mary 2 maintains the transatlantic traditions started in Liverpool on 4 July 1840, when Sir Samuel Cunard left the Mersey aboard the paddle steamer Britannia bound for Halifax, Nova Scotia and Boston.

September 2011 will mark the latest chapter in the history of the Line and the city with the maiden call of Queen Elizabeth and the spectacular return of Queen Mary 2.

Like every call by a Cunard ship since QE2's triumphant first appearance on the Mersey in July 1990, these promise to be days of celebration.

A curtain raiser, perhaps, to 2015 and the 175th anniversary of Britannia setting sail from Liverpool.

*Queen Mary 2 makes her
maiden call at Liverpool
in October 2009*

BUILDING ON HERITAGE

CUNARD LINE'S PARENT COMPANY CARNIVAL CORPORATION AND PLC ANNOUNCED THE INTENTION TO BUILD A NEW CUNARD LINER IN OCTOBER 2008.

The news came a matter of weeks before the world famous and most successful ocean liner in history – Queen Elizabeth 2 – was due to make its final Cunard voyage after being sold to a Middle Eastern consortium based in Dubai.

The timing of the new build announcement, coupled with the fact that the £350m new ship was to be named Queen Elizabeth, sparked immediate speculation that this was to be the successor to the much loved QE2.

Time will be the best judge of that. The new Queen Elizabeth follows in the very long and illustrious wake of her sister ship.

The new ship was constructed using the very latest technology – systems and techniques light years away from the human toil and endeavour that hallmarked the efforts of the workforce at John Brown's yard on the Clyde at Glasgow, where the drawings of naval architects based in the Cunard Building at Liverpool were brought to life late in the 1960s.

Queen Elizabeth is the second Cunarder, after Queen Victoria, to be built in Italy and her sister Queen Mary 2 was herself built in France.

And in the same way as the construction and entry into service of her sister ships represented collaboration and enterprise on a huge scale by a truly international team, so Queen Elizabeth owes her creation to the efforts and skills of a truly diverse group spanning dozens of nationalities.

The order to build was placed with Italian shipbuilders Fincantieri, whose yards have a track record of building ships for various Carnival brands including Holland America Line, P & O Cruises, Princess, and Carnival Cruise Line itself.

Just two years before being awarded the Queen Elizabeth contract, Fincantieri has successfully completed and delivered Queen Victoria to Cunard Line. The Italian conglomerate was delighted to win such a prestigious second order for the most famous shipping company in the world and set about its task immediately.

The first major decision for the build team was where the ship would be built. Queen Victoria has been constructed at the company's Marghera yard near Venice. Schedules and capacity dictated a switch for the new build Queen Elizabeth.

The latest Cunarder would come to life at the firm's Monfalcone yard near Trieste.

On Thursday 2 July, a ceremony to mark the Keel Laying was held at the shipyard. The keel laying involved the placement in the dry dock of the first section of the ship's hull. This section was made up of six pre-manufactured blocks, weighing 364 tons and pre-fitted with 104 tons of pipes, cables, insulation and other equipment.

The ceremony followed an intensive period of design and development.

A total of 53 sections were used in the construction of Queen Elizabeth.

The assembly of these huge sections, and the fitting out of the ship would be completed in a little over two years.

Top: Queen Elizabeth's keel is laid
Centre: Carol Marlow, then President of Cunard, at the ceremony
Bottom: The Queen Elizabeth taking shape

Paolo Capobianco of shipbuilders Fincantieri, at the keel-laying ceremony

Paolo Capobianco, Fincantieri Shipyard Director, commented: "Our Company is the heir to the Italian shipbuilding industry and the world leader in cruise ship construction, and believes, as Cunard does, in the possibility and the need of actively matching tradition and innovation.

"Building a new liner for Cunard is a special achievement for Fincantieri and takes us right to our roots, fostering both our determination to build once again a passenger ship of high technological content and unmistakable style, reflecting the best of the industry and tailored to the needs and requirements of the ship owner."

Before the historic Keel Laying ceremony, Queen Elizabeth's build had already been marked by a major milestone.

Anticipation of her delivery end entry into Cunard Line service was widespread.

On 1 April the new Liner's maiden voyage went on sale. In an astonishing 29 minutes and 14 seconds it was completely sold out. More than 50% of the remaining Maiden Season voyages also sold out within one and a half hours.

Carol Marlow, then Cunard Line's President and Managing Director, commented: "This Maiden Voyage sold out quicker, and involved more guests, than QE2's Final Voyage when it went on sale in June 2007, setting a record then of 36 minutes. This is an impressive record set by what will be an impressive ship and speaks volumes for the Cunard brand as well as for the resilience of the cruise sector as a whole in these challenging times. It has also been very encouraging to see the level of interest in Queen Elizabeth coming from all our international markets with bookings from the UK, US and Germany particularly strong."

With the setting of such a record, the design and build team knew their efforts would soon come under close scrutiny from excited – but generally discerning – guests.

In September 2009, Captain Christopher Wells was announced and appointed as Master of the new vessel. The following January, attention switched back to the yard where the new ship was prepared to be floated for the first time.

Special ceremonies were planned at the yard.

Cunard's current President and Managing Director, Peter Shanks, was joined by 79-year-old Florence (Dennie) Farmer as guest of honour at the event. Dennie's husband, Willie Farmer joined Cunard in September 1938 and served as Chief Engineer on both Queen Elizabeth and QE2 until retirement in October 1979.

Since her husband's death Dennie has sailed with Cunard many times and her link to the two previous Queen Elizabeth ships is unparalleled. In recognition of this, Cunard bestowed on Dennie the honour – in Italian tradition – of being 'Madrina' to the third Queen Elizabeth.

The first ceremony involved the welding of significant coins beneath the mast of Queen Elizabeth for good luck. Three coins were chosen – a half crown dated 1938 (the year the first Queen Elizabeth was launched); a sovereign dated 1967 (the year QE2 was launched) and a sovereign dated 2010 to acknowledge the fact that the new Queen Elizabeth was floated out in 2010. After the coin ceremony, the focus moved to the dockside where the ship was blessed, and a bottle of Italian prossecco was smashed against the hull by the Madrina.

The valves of the dry dock then opened so the ship met the water for the first time.

During the formal ceremony, Peter Shanks told guests: "It is only a little over six months since the keel for this great ship was laid.

"In that short time a solitary block at the bottom of the dry dock has, as a result of the skill and discipline of the workforce here at Fincantieri, grown into this awe-inspiring vessel.

"Even in her present unfinished state, devoid of the carpets and curtains, furnishings and facilities, paintings and porcelain that we associate with a Cunard luxury liner, she is awesome. Of our 170 years of history there has been an 'Elizabeth' in the fleet for over 70, and this ship – the second largest Cunarder ever built –will take the name far into the 21st Century".

Four months later in May, attention on Queen Elizabeth returned to the UK where a special reception was held at the London Showrooms of Viscount David Linley, nephew of the Queen.

Tireless toil to build the new Cunarder

Queen Elizabeth's luxurious public dining rooms during fitting out

Cunard ships, while among the most modern afloat, are known for their traditional luxury, accentuated by extensive use of brass, classic fabrics, marble and highly polished woods and veneers.

So the interior of Queen Elizabeth posed a particular challenge for designers deciding how to treat the significant central arched space on the sweeping staircase leading up from the main deck in the ship's soaring Grand Lobby, the first area to greet embarking passengers.

Peter Shanks recalled: "We needed to fill that space with a decorative screen which would not just be dramatic, a 'wow' factor in an area already full of 'wow', but which would also reflect our emphasis on traditional and sumptuous materials.

"After much thought and exploratory work, it was decided to commission a 5.6-metre (18 ft 6 in) high marquetry panel depicting the original Queen Elizabeth, an Art Deco icon, using a variety of natural woods from around the world.

"Once we had decided on the theme and the medium, it didn't take us long to conclude that

no-one was better qualified for this detailed but monumental work than the company of the exceptional craftsman David Linley, whose creative ability and mastery of wood is renowned".

As a result, Linley, a company specialising in the design and manufacture of fine furniture and marquetry was commissioned to design and make this stunning centrepiece at the heart of the ship.

Work was completed at the Linley workshops in the UK and the giant piece was packed for shipment to Italy and installation.

The hanging and installation took four days to complete.

The magnificent artwork shows the port bow of the original Queen Elizabeth seen dramatically from sea level, and is intricately executed using

the technique of marquetry inlay in nine different types of wood veneers.

Spanning 2½ decks, the panel is made up of nine panels seamlessly jointed to lightweight board.

The marquetry panel features Madrona, Indian ebony, American walnut, grey ripple sycamore, burr ash, bird's eye maple, satin walnut , ash, burr walnut and Macassar ebony – all used to depict the evocative image of Queen Elizabeth.

Commenting on the challenges faced by the bespoke commission, Linley's Chairman, David Linley, who founded the company in 1985, said: "Though we have made fittings for luxury yachts in the past, this was the first sea-going work we have done on this scale – it is certainly the largest screen we have ever made – but it was a commission I was delighted to accept. I recall my father saying the interior design on Cunard's Queen Elizabeth 2 made one proud to be British, so I am hoping our achievement on the new Queen Elizabeth will make him – and others – equally proud".

The screen was one of the final major artworks to be installed on board the ship before it was ready to be handed over to its new owners.

Cunard Line took delivery of Queen Elizabeth – the second largest Cunarder ever and the third new liner the company has built in six years – on 30 September 2010.

The Linley Panel in the Grand Lobby

The Handover Ceremony took place on board the vessel at the Fincantieri shipyard. The event included the ceremonial lowering of the Italian flag and the raising of the Blue Ensign in recognition of Captain Christopher Wells' service in the Royal Naval Reserve.

Peter Shanks said: "This ceremony to mark the completion of the ship, and our acceptance of delivery, marked the start of a number of significant events culminating in the ship's official naming by Her Majesty The Queen."

The new ship – and most of its crew who had been on board preparing the ship for Cunard's renowned White Star Service – left Venice the same day bound for her home port of Southampton.

The Grand Lobby

ART DECO CLASS

The Queens Room

AS BEFITS A LINER BEARING SUCH A NAME, QUEEN ELIZABETH OFFERS THE ESSENCE OF INTERIOR STYLE AND SOPHISTICATION – WITH THE MODERN TWISTS OF INDIVIDUALITY NOT AVAILABLE TO THE DESIGNERS OF HER ILLUSTRIOUS PREDECESSOR.

Art deco flourishes, rich wood panelling, intricate mosaics, gleaming chandeliers, and cool marbles combine to give Queen Elizabeth a unique design and personality of her own – a style that reflects that found on her sister ocean liners Queen Mary 2 and Queen Victoria.

All three ships offer elegant public rooms that combine grand spaces and intimate public areas.

Queen Elizabeth impresses as soon as guests embark into the ship's triple height Grand Lobby which shows the grandeur of the ship and links her with ocean liners of the past.

With its finishes of light mahogany and marble, a stunning art deco chandelier from the era of the first Queen Elizabeth, cantilevered balconies and a magnificent two-deck-high original artwork piece by Viscount Linley on the grand staircase, the Grand Lobby is the social focal point of the ship. Cunard Line guests experience some of the finest dining at sea in restaurants assigned to their choice of accommodation, or stateroom.

On Queen Elizabeth, restaurants follow a similar pattern to Cunard's other ships, with Grill Rooms for the higher suites and a main restaurant for the deluxe grades. The ship also has a Britannia Club for the top grade balcony guests.

Queen Elizabeth's Britannia Club restaurant is an exclusive sea view dining room with art deco touches and a striking, colourful decorative ceiling featuring backlit glass panels and a sand-blasted decorative art deco glass wall.

The main dining room, the Britannia Restaurant, is one of the most remarkable rooms at sea, spanning two decks at the stern of the vessel and offering a true art deco feel. It evokes memories of classic ocean liner restaurants with a unique sweeping staircase.

Both the Queens Grill and Princess Grills are located at the top of the ship on Deck 11, enclosed by graceful and gently curving panoramic glass walls on the seaboard sides, and cantilevered out over the side of the vessel above Deck 10.

Britannia Restaurant

Although architecturally similar, the restaurants themselves are differently decorated to create an individual feel.

Grills guests have exclusive use of their own private lounge and bar conveniently located next to the Grills restaurants, complete with resident Concierge.

French–style doors open from each Grill onto the Courtyard – an exclusive patio area, where al fresco dining is offered, and steps lead up to the Grills Terrace – a secluded retreat on the ship's uppermost deck where Grills guests can enjoy luxurious sun beds and exclusive waiter service.

In addition Queen Elizabeth offers several alternative dining venues.

The Verandah Grills on board the original Queen Mary and Queen Elizabeth were perhaps the most exclusive dining rooms at sea, on a par with exclusive private clubs in London, New York and Paris.

These Grills were available to first-class passengers who wanted a truly exclusive experience and the rooms would be frequented by royalty, film stars, the rich and the famous.

In keeping with this tradition, The Verandah on Queen Elizabeth offers fine cuisine, contemporary design and impeccable service. The Verandah is a light and elegant room with artwork inspired by the murals on board the first two Queens, where vintage menus tell the story of the dining experience on board the original Queen Elizabeth.

The Garden Lounge, also named after a room on the first Queen Elizabeth, hosts occasional evening Supper Clubs with musical entertainment and dancing.

The area has a palm–filled conservatory feel inspired by the glass houses at Kew Gardens and its vaulted glass ceiling making it a truly light, bright and airy place to sit by day.

Queen Elizabeth's Lido Restaurants on Deck 9 are light and spacious areas with wonderful sea views, offering breakfast and lunch buffet style. In the evenings South American cuisine is offered in 'Asado', Mexican dishes are served in

Above:
The Garden Lounge,
night and day

Right: The Verandah
Grill Restaurant

'Aztec' while 'Jasmine' offers Asian fare.

The extensive Café Carinthia on Deck 2 continues the popular concept introduced on Queen Victoria and offers art deco style and rich décor whilst guests can enjoy sweet pastries and fine teas and coffees. Another Cunard tradition, the Golden Lion pub, offers traditional English pub food for lunch in a typical British pub setting.

Stylish entertainment venues are another hallmark of the Cunard fleet. On Queen Elizabeth, the magnificent three-deck Royal Court Theatre, with tiered seating for 832 guests, is the location for the main entertainment of the evening with full-scale, West End-style productions, by the Queen Elizabeth Theatre Company, as well as named entertainers.

Decorated in a regal blue and gold colour scheme, this grand auditorium offers private boxes on the upper level along with a lounge area for guests to enjoy drinks before the show.

They can then enjoy champagne and petit fours or chocolates in their box during the show,

ringing for service as they wish on their private (and silent!) velvet bell pull.

Queen Elizabeth's two-deck Queens Room, another Cunard signature feature, is designed for dancing, cocktail parties and traditional English afternoon teas complete with finger sandwiches and freshly baked scones with jam and cream.

This glorious room highlights Cunard's royal links and traditions and has murals inspired by views from royal palaces. Other highlights are the dramatic high ceiling, crystal chandeliers, a large 1000 sq ft dance floor with inlaid wood patterns and rich wall décor, with spectacular art deco glass panels.

Queen Elizabeth's forward Games Deck, named after the same space on the original Queen Elizabeth, offers paddle tennis, croquet and bowls under a canopy to shield players from the sun. The bowls green is appropriate given the fact that Queen Elizabeth's home port of Southampton houses the oldest surviving bowls green in the world, first used in 1299!

Above:
The Royal Court Theatre, left, showing the art deco theatre boxes.

Below:
Forward games deck

Above: Midships bar exhibiting memorabilia from the original Queen Elizabeth

Below: The Fortnum & Mason store on board

The original Queen Elizabeth is further celebrated in the Midships Bar on Deck 3 in a space named after one of the more popular spaces on the original ship. Cabinets house memorabilia from that liner with the artwork typical of the 1930s and 1940s.

Queen Elizabeth offers a whole range of bars and clubs to suit a wide variety of tastes and provide a range of atmospheres, including the traditional English Pub, a nautically-themed observation lounge (Commodore Club) and the Yacht Club which is named after the lively entertainment space found aft on QE2 offering

guests the perfect venue for activities and gatherings during the day or dancing at night, with views from its 270 degrees of windows.

The Yacht Club also has on display several famous pieces from QE2 including the silver model which was centrepiece in that ship's Midships Lobby.

The very traditional Royal Arcade on Decks 2 and 3 presents famous brand names, such as Fortnum & Mason, Hackett, Harris Tweed and Anya Hindmarch, in 4000 sq ft of shops while the two-tiered Library features a unique leaded glass ceiling and a globe from the era of Cunard's first Queen Elizabeth, along with a 6,000 volume book collection.

The 'Cunarders' Gallery' displays captioned black and white photography of previous Cunard celebrity guests on Cunard liners while 'Cunard Place' displays memorabilia from previous Cunard liners as well as special exhibits.

Child facilities on board Queen Elizabeth are on Deck 10. The Play Zone and The Zone feature the very latest equipment for children of all ages. A permanent staff and nursery nurses are on hand in this inside / outside play area.

Health and fitness facilities for adults are extensive. The Cunard Royal Spa and Fitness Centre feature the latest spa and beauty treatments for both men and women, as well as a hydro-pool and thermal suite.

Below: Commodore Club

Forward of the Spa is the expansive gymnasium and aerobics area with state-of-the-art cardiovascular fitness equipment including inclining treadmills and bikes complete with their own personal LCD television screens.

In addition to the large hydro-pool in the Spa, there are two outdoor swimming pools on Deck 9 and a large aft sunbathing area.

Queen Elizabeth has 1,046 staterooms of which 892 (85%) are outside staterooms with 738 (71%) featuring balconies.

There are 127 Grills Suites on Queen Elizabeth, twinned with dining in the Grills restaurants, and offering the ultimate in suite accommodation at sea. For the first time the six main Queens Grill suites are named after the six Cunard Commodores who have been knighted: Commodore Sir Arthur Rostron, Commodore Sir Edgar Britten, Commodore Sir Ivan Thompson, Commodore Sir Cyril Illingworth; Commodore Sir James Bisset and Commodore Sir James Charles. Each suite features a portrait and biography of the Commodore after whom it is named.

There are nine different types of suites and staterooms: Grand Suites, Master Suites, Penthouses, Queens Suites, Princess Suites, Britannia Club, Balcony, Outside and Inside.

Above: Relaxing in the Royal Spa

*Wake up in the city that never sleeps –
the Queen Mary 2 sails past the vivid
skyline of New York*

QM2 – A CITY AT SEA

AS THE LARGEST, LONGEST, WIDEST, TALLEST AND MOST EXPENSIVE NORTH ATLANTIC LINER EVER BUILT, THERE IS NO MISTAKING QUEEN MARY 2.

Some believe it takes a famous port landmark like the Statue of Liberty or a city waterfront like the Sydney Opera House and its neighbour the Harbour Bridge to bring some meaning to the scale of the vessel. Liverpool placed itself firmly on that list after the ship's maiden call in October 2009.

Those who witness the vessel from the outside in any such surroundings only see half the story. If the outside is impressive the inside is simply stunning – thanks in no small part to the sheer volume of space made available to Queen Mary 2's interior designers. This allowed Cunard to produce a variety of guest spaces – grand, elegant, imposing, intimate and, in some cases, quite revolutionary.

The Grand Lobby is the point of embarkation for the majority of guests whether travelers or day visitors. This six-storey high space is dominated by a striking winged-staircase and dramatic works of art – part of more than £3m worth of art on board.

The main Dining Room, the Britannia Restaurant (seating 1,347 guests), is one of the most remarkable rooms at sea, spanning the full width of the ship and nearly three stories in height with tiered dining on two levels.

It evokes memories of classic ocean liner restaurants with a sweeping central staircase – perfect for those who wish to make a grand entrance – an overhead light well and classic columns. A vast tapestry of a past Cunard liner hangs as a centrepiece.

The 200-seat Queens Grill, decorated in gold, is for the use of guests booked in the highest-grade staterooms and features the finest dining afloat. These guests also have the exclusive use of the Queens Grill Bar (conveniently located next to the Grill) and the outdoor Queens Grill Terrace. The intimate 178-seat Princess Grill, decorated in silver, is for guests in the Junior Suite staterooms.

In addition Queen Mary 2 offers several alternative dining venues.

The 156-seat Todd English Restaurant is branded after a renowned US culinary icon and offers innovative Mediterranean cuisine in a modern setting. The room has been designed with intimate alcoves and architectural detailing and overlooks the Pool Terrace allowing for al fresco dining.

The six-storey high space of the Grand Lobby on the QM2 (top), and the remarkable Britannia Restaurant

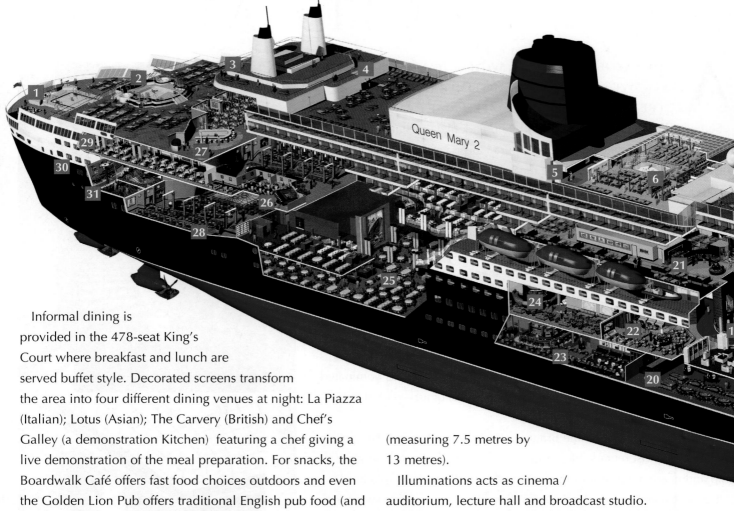

Informal dining is provided in the 478-seat King's Court where breakfast and lunch are served buffet style. Decorated screens transform the area into four different dining venues at night: La Piazza (Italian); Lotus (Asian); The Carvery (British) and Chef's Galley (a demonstration Kitchen) featuring a chef giving a live demonstration of the meal preparation. For snacks, the Boardwalk Café offers fast food choices outdoors and even the Golden Lion Pub offers traditional English pub food (and beers) for lunch!

The Royal Court Theatre, with tiered seating for 1,094, is a full-scale, West End-style theatre with production capacity to match.

Lavish stage shows and featured entertainers can be enjoyed in supreme comfort by Royal Court audiences.

Classically elegant in style, this stunning theatre has a hydraulic proscenium stage and highly sophisticated light and sound equipment as well as excellent sight-lines.

Queen Mary 2's Queens Room is the largest ballroom at sea and is designed for ballroom dancing, cocktail parties and afternoon teas.

It features a dramatic high ceiling (more than seven metres high), crystal chandeliers, sweeping ocean views on both sides of the ship and the largest dance floor at sea

(measuring 7.5 metres by 13 metres).

Illuminations acts as cinema / auditorium, lecture hall and broadcast studio. Perhaps even more exciting is the fact that the room also hosts the first Planetarium at sea featuring high-tech programmes and virtual reality films. The planetarium "dome" can be lowered for would be star-gazers to enjoy a tour of the nigh sky.

ConneXions is a unique education centre featuring seven flexible classroom venues for Cunard's enrichment programme. Classes in everything from Computer Training, Seamanship and Navigation to Art and Wine Appreciation, Languages and Photography are taught by expert instructors during voyages.

The Winter Garden acts as Queen Mary 2's 'quiet area' and is reminiscent if a grand conservatory with flowers in bloom all year long, aroma management, a large waterfall and a piano – a popular venue for the serving of Cunard's

---

QM2 AT A GLANCE

1 Minnows Pool	10 Atlantic Room	19 Grand Lobby	28 Queens Room - Ballroom
2 Terrace Pool	11 Commodore Club Lounge	20 Empire Casino	29 Queens Grill
3 Grand Duplex & Duplex Apartments	12 Library & Bookshop	21 King's Court Alternative Dining Venues	30 Children's Facilities
4 Broadwalk Café	13 Royal Suites with private access	22 Veuve Clicquot Champagne Bar	31 G32 Nightclub
5 Fairways - Golf Simulators	14 Illuminations - Theatre & Auditorium	23 Golden Lion Pub	*not shown*
6 The Pavilion	15 Canyon Ranch SpaClub	24 Chart Room Bar and Lounge	• May Shops
7 Splash Pool	16 Cunard ConneXions™	25 Britannia Restaurant	• Sir Samual's Wine Bar
8 Sports Centre	17 Royal Court Theatre	26 Queens Grill Lounge	• The Zone & Play Zone children's facilities
9 The Look - Observation Deck	18 Winter Garden Lounge	27 Todd English Restaurant	• Princess Grill
			• Regatta Bar
			• Churchill's Cigar Lounge

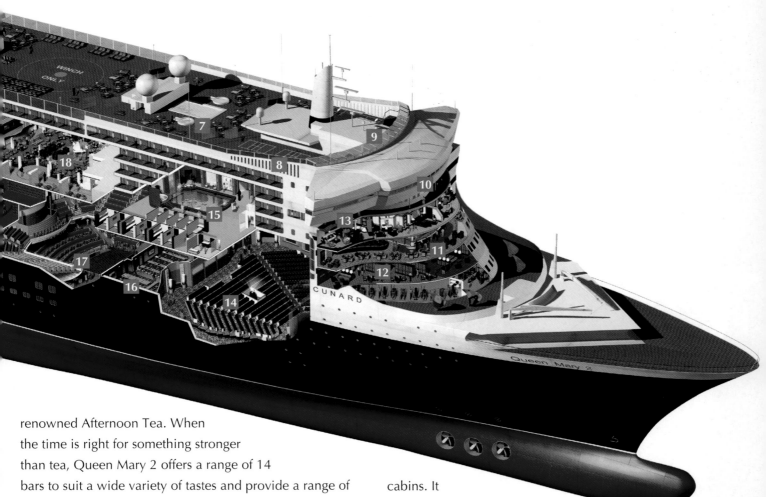

renowned Afternoon Tea. When the time is right for something stronger than tea, Queen Mary 2 offers a range of 14 bars to suit a wide variety of tastes and provide a range of atmospheres.

These include a traditional English Pub (the Golden Lion), an up-market modern Wine Bar (Sir Samuel's), a nautically-themed cocktail bar (The Chart Room) and the Veuve Clicquot Champagne Bar. A Terrace Bar and a Regatta Bar serve those enjoying being on the open decks.

Queen Mary 2's G32 Nightclub is named after the hull number given to the ship by her builders and is strategically situated overlooking the stern of the ship, away from guest cabins. It uses state-of-the-art technology as well as featuring an interesting two-point entrance and mezzanine level.

The forward Commodore Club observation lounge offers sweeping views over the bow of Queen Mary 2 and features jazz each evening. Connected to this room are the Boardroom and Cigar Lounge. The Library and Bookshop, situated forward, is the largest to be found at sea and is an extremely popular venue with comfortable leather sofas and

Trip the light fantastic with dazzling entertainment on board Queen Mary 2

armchairs. The library offers 8,000 hardbacks, 500 paperbacks, 200 audio books and 100 CD ROMs and is staffed by full-time librarians.

Children have not been forgotten and facilities on board Queen Mary 2 are among the finest afloat. The Play Zone and The Zone features the very latest equipment for children of all ages. Children have their own dedicated pool and inside / outside play area.

For those interested in the history of Cunard, 'Maritime Quest' is a museum quality audio tour of the ship that tells the story of the most famous name in shipping.

Health and fitness facilities are among the largest and most extensive ever to be featured on board a ship.

Covering 20,000 square feet on two decks, the Queen Mary 2 Spa is operated by the critically acclaimed Canyon Ranch brand.

The Spa offers services previously only found in luxurious, elite establishments ashore, and is of such quality that some guests choose to sail on this ship for its spa facilities alone!

There is also a complete gymnasium, Thalassotherapy pool, whirlpool, herbal sauna, Finnish sauna, reflexology basins and an aromatic steam room. 51 Canyon Ranch staff are on hand to assist in the 24 treatment rooms and other facilities.

Renowned international artists were commissioned to produce over 300 works of art from a trompe l'oeil painted ceiling in the Winter Garden to a huge tapestry in the Britannia Restaurant to a monumental sculptural relief in the Grand Lobby.

Other than the large indoor pool in the Spa, there are four swimming pools outside. One of these can be covered by a retractable sliding glass roof - becoming an additional indoor pool if required.

Towering over 200 feet above sea level the

sports facilities include two state-of-the-art golf simulators, a half-size basketball court, putting green, quoits, shuffleboard, deck games, a giant chess board and a paddle tennis court. There are eight whirlpool tubs (2 variable, 5 outdoor and 1 indoor)

Interior promenades circling several decks provide additional attractive walking venues.

Another classic feature is the expansive Promenade Deck, recreating an area which always served an important social function aboard transatlantic liners.

This deck allows a 360° passage around the ship, protected from the weather at the forward end.

One lap of The Promenade circuit is just over one third of a mile. This generous deck can accommodate a line of full-length wooden steamer chairs, and still leave room for guests walking four abreast to pass between the seated guests and the rail.

In case it's needed, Queen Mary 2's medical facility is one of the largest and most modern of its kind in the world

Other Shipboard amenities include a Beauty Salon, Currency Exchange Bank, Dry Cleaning & Laundry Service; Concierge Service and a Florist.

In short – Cunard's grandest city at sea.

A life on the ocean wave – from top; enjoying the view from a balcony stateroom aboard Queen Mary 2; the Pavilion Pool; the children's Play Zone

CUNARD AT THE HEART OF LIVERPOOL

LIVERPOOL HAD TO WAIT A LONG TIME FOR THE ARRIVAL OF A CUNARD QUEEN IN THE MERSEY – BUT THOSE WHO WITNESSED THE EVENT SAY IT WAS WORTH THE WAIT.

The Line's former worldwide headquarters at Cunard Building – resplendent after a lavish external refurbishment – had long since passed into new hands and multiple tenancy when, on 24 July 1990, the distinctive brick-red funnel of a Cunarder was once again visible on the Mersey. And this was no lesser Cunarder then Queen Elizabeth 2 making her first call at her spiritual home.

Much of the design work and negotiations with her builders were completed inside the Cunard Building – now an iconic focal point of Liverpool's UNESCO World Heritage Site. Built during the First World War, the middle of Liverpool's Three Graces – so named after the daughters of Zeus who personified grace, beauty and charm – was the final building of the three to be completed.

Today, although the interior of the building has been sub-let to various companies and organisations, there is no mistaking the purpose for which it was designed and built.

As well as being a ticketing office and embarkation hall for the passenger line, it also housed Cunard's complete shore-based teams of designers, engineers and managers who ran the global operation from the Mersey waterfront.

The building's historic maritime pedigree offers a fascinating insight into how Liverpool was once established as a focal point of world passenger trade.

The ground floor main hall served as the main passenger embarkation facility where guests exited by the imposing entrance straight on to Pier Head and their waiting Liner.

The building was constructed on the site of the former George's Dock and a section of Liverpool's original sea wall has been retained deep in the basement of the building. Elsewhere in the basement, huge vaults, each named after a serving Cunard Liner, were used for the safekeeping of passengers' valuables.

Huge luggage storage areas are also retained with row upon row of wooden shelving still bearing the names of famous Cunard ships. On the top floor of the building a magnificent hall was reserved for the use of First Class passengers who could enjoy afternoon tea dances while waiting for their Liners to be readied.

The QE2, in the River Mersey for the last time, berths at the Pier Head in Liverpool

The building is made of reinforced concrete, clad in Portland stone. The frieze is carved with the shields of countries allied in the First World War. A stately marble-lined corridor with Doric columns links the North and South entrances, giving access to lifts and stairs.

The Cunard Building was the centre of Britain's cruise ship industry for many years, a land based reflection of the glory and wealth of cruise liners. Its design was influenced by grand Italian palaces and reflects the Greek neo-classical revival.

In the forecourt of the Cunard Building is the company's war memorial; a slender column on top of which is a bronze figure of VICTORY. Above the doors leading directly to the waterfront there remains a large lion rampant on a globe – Cunard Line's emblem.

That first visit by QE2 drew an estimated 1 million people to the banks of the Mersey. Subsequent calls – nine in total – together with the more recent, spectacular arrivals of QE2's sister ships Queen Mary 2 and Queen Victoria, have renewed the strong associations between Cunard and the City of Liverpool. In the space of a week during September 2011 these links will become stronger still with visits by Queen Elizabeth and the return of Queen Mary 2.

That now famous 1990 visit was a momentous day for Cunard Line and Liverpool, coming exactly 150 years after Sir Samuel Cunard's transatlantic service was launched when the paddle steamer Britannia left the Mersey bound for Halifax, Nova Scotia and Boston.

Just as the departure of Britannia had captured the imagination of the city on 4 July 1840, so the arrival of the most famous ship in the world triggered a day and night of celebration on both banks of the river – and, for those lucky enough to experience them, a series of lavish celebratory events on board.

The perfect summer's day has gone down in local history as one of the city's most memorable. It started early for a group of VIP's ushered into a waiting area at the RAF base at Woodvale near Southport. Soon they were climbing aboard a helicopter to be flown out to meet the ship close to the Mersey Bar. After their short flight passengers caught their first glimpse of the mighty liner heading for Liverpool.

The helicopter touched down on board and excited guests disembarked their aircraft to begin their momentous voyage up the Mersey. Civic leaders and other guests received s formal welcome on board.

The previous day, during this special passage commemorating the Line's 150th anniversary, QE2 had called at Cobh in Ireland. Calls at Greenock and Cherbourg were to follow the Liverpool stop as the commemorative tour of the UK and Ireland headed back to Southampton. On the bridge, officers reached for their binoculars to view Crosby beach and soon realised this was to be a very special day.

Thousands of well-wishers were already lining the shore to greet the ship. Similar scenes were visible across the river towards Fort Perch Rock at New Brighton and all the way along the promenade to Seacombe. As the crowds gathered ashore, the river became busy too as a flotilla of small craft turned out to add their welcome.

QE2 was to drop anchor mid river, opposite the Cunard Building where a tender service was to be operated by Mersey Ferries bringing passengers ashore at Pier Head. Tugs deployed to assist played a spectacular part in the welcome by firing their water jets in salute to the liner as she edged closer to her mooring for the day.

As more helicopters and other light aircraft buzzed above, the scene was set for a memorable day of celebration. By lunchtime, the numbers lining the river at Pier Head were swelled by hundreds of office workers drawn to the water's edge to catch a glimpse of the ship.

Impromptu picnics and parties started on both sides of the river as families enjoyed he sunshine and the spectacle.

The Mersey Ferries were packed for each of their special cruises throughout the day and tickets for an evening excursion to coincide with QE2's departure had sold out weeks before.

At lunchtime, ferry passengers witnessed the spectacular release of 10,000 balloons from the ship's Quarter Deck to mark he inaugural call at Liverpool.

As the day unfolded, more and more people made their way to the waterside and by the time the ship was ready to depart at around 11pm the stage was set for a spectacular firework display.

Queen Victoria sails past the Antony Gormley statues in Crosby, on her way into Liverpool in July 2010; Queen Mary 2 with Birkenhead's terraced streets as a backdrop in 2009; New Brighton lighthouse greets QE2 in 2008

With a medley of Beatles songs and a rousing replay of Gerry Marsden's famous anthem Ferry 'Cross the Mersey, QE2 weighed anchor and edged slowly away from her positions in front of the Pier Head.

Thousands of flashguns popped as the final fireworks lit the sky and the ship saluted the city with a several blasts on her whistle.

Some 23 years had passed since Cunard Line closed its former Liverpool headquarters, and it had taken the same time for the Line's flagship to make her maiden call at her spiritual home.

During her eight further calls at the city QE2 continued to captivate crowds on both sides of the Mersey and on the beaches of Wirral and Sefton.

Two of these visits took on extra significance.

In 2007 the legendary liner made a celebratory "Lap of Honour" round Britain voyage to mark the 40th anniversary of her launch. During the afternoon of the call Liverpool Cathedral hosted a concert performed in front of the ship's passengers and other local guests.

A little over a year later it was time for Liverpool to say goodbye to its favourite adopted ship.

QE2 arrived in the Mersey off the Pier Head a little after 11am on Friday, 3rd October 2008, marking the start of a day of celebration and sad farewells.

In line with maritime custom QE2 flew her magnificent 39 foot long paying-off pennant from her mast as her Master Captain Ian McNaught, assisted by a Liverpool Pilot, edged the liner towards her Liverpool berth for the last time.

The pennant is the longest in Cunard Line history – one foot for each year the famous liner was in service. Later that day it was presented to the city of Liverpool during a special farewell concert at the Anglican Cathedral.

QE2's final farewell that evening was watched by tens of thousands of spectators on both sides of the River Mersey – out to witness the end of another chapter in the enduring 170-year history linking Liverpool and Cunard Line.

The next chapter opened a little more than a year later.

On Tuesday 20th October 2009, Liverpool prepared to welcome the largest ocean liner in the world.

Cunard Line's flagship Queen Mary 2 was to make her inaugural call at the city as part of a fifth birthday lap of honour circumnavigation of the British Isles.

She let go her ropes at Southampton's Ocean terminal shortly after 5pm the previous Thursday afternoon bound for South Queensferry in the Firth of Forth near Edinburgh.

Tugs at the Liner's homeport joined the celebrations by providing a fire hose salute as the mighty Cunarder reversed away from her berth into Southampton water

It was a first leg voyage of 460 nautical miles. Throughout

Friday Commodore Bernard Warner and his Bridge team navigated a course close to famous east coast landmarks and resorts along the shore of Yorkshire and Northumberland.

Off spurn Head, at the mouth of the River Humber, QM2 took a course towards the famous Flamborough Head and, beyond, Scarborough.

Strong winds and a heavy sea prevented many small private and pleasure craft from joining the sail past, but ashore thousands of well-wishers were visible from QM2's vast open decks. Car headlights flashed and horns were sounded as the liner made her majestic way north.

Long blasts on the ship's whistle punctuated the passage along the famous stretch of coastline. At Whitby crowds could be seen in the grounds of the resort's famous cliff top ruins while at nearby Sandsend more crowds had waited patiently on the beach to view the ship.

The vessel passed the distinctive twin quays at the mouth of the River Tyne shortly before sunset on Friday evening and helicopters and light aircraft followed her course north.

The Farne Islands, off Bamburgh in Northumberland came and went as QM2 continued her progress towards the Forth.

At sunrise on the Saturday QM2 was nearing her anchorage in the shadow of the famous Forth Railway Bridge at South Queensferry.

Throughout the day, thousands of spectators descended on the waterfront to catch sight of the liner during only her second call at the Edinburgh landmark.

Shortly after 6pm the order was given for the ship to set off for Greenock, a distance of 594 nautical miles.

The following day was spent in spectacular coastal scenery. Early in the morning, QM2 rounded Rottery Head on a north-westerly heading towards Duncansby Head, entering Pentland Firth and passing between the Island of Stroma and South Ronaldsay.

Shortly after breakfast the island of Hoy, dominated by the famous Old Man of Hoy, came into view. The ship then headed towards Cape Wrath before entering the North Minch, passing between the Isle of Lewis and the west coast of Scotland. A short time later, in brilliant sunshine QM2, entered the Little Minch between the Isle of Harris and Isle of Skye and onwards towards the Hebrides.

The following morning, Queen Mary 2 arrived on the Clyde – scene over the years of more than 120 Cunard liner launches.

Before sunrise at Greenock thousands of well-wishers had gathered to welcome the ship on her maiden call. As day broke they were joined by dozens of small craft on the waters around the ships' berth at Clydeport.

That evening, QM2 departed the Clyde, former home to the famous shipyards of John Brown.

Queen Victoria gets ready to leave Liverpool after her visit in July 2010

Glasgow's place in Cunard history is firmly established and survives despite the fact the last liner in the fleet to be built there was QE2, launched off John Brown's slipway by Her Majesty the Queen in September 1967.

Once again, tens of thousands of spectators lined the promenade of the proud industrial town as the mighty, 148,000 ton flagship set off bound for Liverpool. Pipers on the dockside were drowned out by another firework spectacular, greeted with loud cheers from QM2's packed open decks and the crowded vantage points ashore.

On board that evening the sense of excitement about the following day's arrival in Liverpool grew.

By the time most guests surfaced from their staterooms for breakfast (or had enjoyed their first meal of the day as room service) QM2 was making good speed off the Anglesey coast.

The weather was fair with a stiff breeze across the open decks. On the bridge Commodore Bernard Warner – making his first call by ship to the port of Liverpool – and his team prepared for the spectacular arrival at Pier Head. Plans had

been drawn up for the longest, widest, tallest (and grandest!) ocean liner in the world to turn in mid Mersey to berth "starboard on" at Liverpool. Painstaking calculations of tidal range and depth of water had also been made – in the first instance to make sure the huge ship could pass the Mersey Bar safely and then to ensure she could be safely tied up at the berth.

Intensive dredging of the river bed around the berth had been carried out in the days before the visit.

Before the ship reached that final resting point for the day she had to pass through a flotilla of welcoming craft. Tugs, Lifeboats, speed boats, private launches, jet skis and a packed Mersey Ferry Royal Daffodil passed as close as they dare to the mighty liner as she made her way between Crosby beach and Fort Perch Rock at New Brighton.

The Wirral promenade was thronged with spectators and light aircraft and film helicopters buzzed overhead.

Tugs in attendance switched on their fire hoses in salute – at one stage drenching unsuspecting passengers on the liner's open decks.

With one of the highest and fastest flowing tidal ranges in Britain the Mersey commands both concentration and respect from those navigating its waters.

Commodore Warner and his team had worked with Liverpool Pilot Chris Booker to plan the arrival – and the intricate mid-river turn.

On board the first signs that the turn was underway became apparent sooner than many guests had expected.

Shortly after passing Wallasey Town Hall and the Wirral promenade at Egremont, those paying attention on board became aware of what those ashore could see for themselves: the giant liner was turning.

The manoeuvre was a complex piece of expert seamanship delivered to perfection. With the tide running at four knots, QM2 was allowed to drift gently to the landing stage.

By 1145 she was alongside and secure a short while later marking the start of another remarkable day for Cunard and the City of Liverpool.

Peter Shanks later offered his own reflections on the historic day.

"It was hard to imagine after the spectacular departure from Greenock the night before that things could get any better – but they did.

"My start to the day was on the bridge as we sailed into the River Mersey. There was a strong tide with us pushing the ship along. As we neared the centre of the city it became clear why the day was going to be so special – many thousands of people had come out to greet us.

"In front of us were the famous Three Graces buildings and from the central building, the Cunard building, flew the Cunard house flag.

"I don't think the people of Liverpool knew what to think as the mammoth Queen Mary 2 performed a perfect 180 degree turn as she came down on the tide – ending up perfectly in line with the berth. I am not sure how many times the ship's whistle blew – but there was no doubting we had arrived."

Liverpool is once again set to host a Cunard spectacular.

Turning to perfection – QM2 on the Mersey

ROYAL VISIT TO THE CITY

JULY 26 2010 MARKED ANOTHER MILESTONE IN THE ENDURING HISTORY OF CUNARD LINE LINKS WITH LIVERPOOL.

As well as marking the first call by Queen Victoria to the Line's spiritual home, the day also included a very important visit for the ship and her company as HRH the Duchess of Cornwall returned to board for the first time since she named the liner at Southampton on 10 December 2007.

The return Royal Visit was to be a highlight of the ship's first round Britain voyage – creating a higher than usual sense of anticipation among guests on board for whom "Liverpool Day" on Cunard voyages around the UK has established itself as a day of celebration and excitement.

Queen Victoria crossed the Mersey Bar around breakfast time with hundreds of guests making an early start to line her open decks.

They were not disappointed by the welcome.

A flotilla of small craft bobbed about a Mersey Ferry laden with sightseers keen to catch a water-borne view of the new Cunarder's arrival.

Aircraft, including a media helicopter, buzzed above while ashore at Crosby, New Brighton, Egremont and Woodside, crowds of spectators undeterred by persistent rain, gathered to witness another piece of maritime history unfold on the Mersey.

Peter Shanks, Cunard Line President and Managing Director, offers his reflections on the day:

"At Cunard we are blessed with special events and very special days. That day on Queen Victoria's Round Britain Voyage, was just such a day. The ingredients were pretty special –a maiden call to our spiritual home of Liverpool, a Royal visit from the ship's Godmother, The Duchess of Cornwall and a celebration of 170 years to the month of the first ever voyage by a Cunard ship, The Britannia from Liverpool to Boston and Halifax in 1840.

"I travelled up to Liverpool the night before and whilst waiting for a taxi to take us down to the port enjoyed some friendly banter with the hotel reception staff. It was pouring with rain and had been for a week, but the powers that be had imposed a hosepipe ban in the city. They should have known better as it rained when QE2 came to the city to say farewell in 2008, it rained when Queen Mary 2 made her maiden visit last year. Fingers crossed for this year's visits by Queen Elizabeth and Queen Mary 2!

"We arrived at a damp and drizzly dockside at 0800. I was not sure what to expect. Queen

Queen Victoria leaves the Mersey

A majestic arrival

Mary 2 had attracted many hundreds of onlookers. I was very pleasantly surprised. The first sight was Queen Victoria going sideways down the river Mersey. There is a strong river tide, so as the ship makes her 180 degree turn to come alongside, the tide continues to push her down the river; quite a sight but I knew that Captain Paul Wright had things under control.

"The second wonderful sight was the many hundreds of Liverpool people who were on the dockside. There is so much pride in Liverpool – it's a fabulous city. And here they were, just yards from the iconic Cunard Building, welcoming a new Cunard Liner into Liverpool for the first time, as many people have done over the last 170 years. Remarkable.

"There was a buzz of excitement in the cruise terminal, not just for the ship, but also for the pending Royal Visit. I was rather amused to see that the band was a ukulele band. I asked the cruise terminal manager why a ukulele band and she said it had worked well recently for a German cruise visit – and do you know what? When they struck-up their first tune – and I have never heard 20 ukulele's all at once – they sang Beatles Songs. Well of course it was going to be Beatles, we were in Liverpool and it was actually rather good and received a huge round of applause from the arriving guests looking on with interest from their balconies.

"The first sign of trouble on boarding the ship was the news that our Godmother, Duchess of Cornwall was going to be an hour late for her visit. Her helicopter had broken down. My first thought was what a good excuse that was. It was marvellous to watch the seamless way in which our on board team calmly set about changing plans for the morning.

"As it happened the Royal Party was only 45 minutes late, but the Duchess stayed with us for the full hour that she had promised and it was really very touching to see her come back to visit her ship and to see so many of our crew.

"On arrival in the Grand Lobby our crew was right around all three levels and gave a very warm welcome.

"The Duchess of Cornwall seemed very at home and happy to be back on board. She unveiled a silver plaque and toured the Galley, meeting many of our chef's and cooks.

"She also visited the Bridge. We had planned that she would blow the ship's whistles across the city at 1200. Problem – it was now 1245. No problem, The Captain announced 'Ma'am – it is precisely 1200, would you care to blow the ship's whistles?' And blow then she did to great effect.

"It was really quite moving to see the beaming faces of so many of the ship's company as they met our Godmother.

"Of course most of them these days have mobile phones with cameras. I am convinced that many of them would be sending their photos home to their families. Our crews are such proud people, and to make their day special was, for me, the absolute highlight of the day. So on we went to The Queens Room where the Duchess met more crew members and some of our guests. It was here we asked our Godmother to cut our birthday cake.

"Yes, our 170th birthday. Amazing to think the paddle steamer Britannia that left the Mersey for the first time in 1840 would have fitted inside the Queen Room we were standing in in 2010, a sign of just how Cunard Line has developed over 170 years.

"Our allocated 55 minutes in a busy day's schedule passed in a flash. As I escorted our Godmother down the gangway I thanked her for coming and explained how much the Ship's Company appreciated her coming back to see her ship.

"If that was not enough for one day, later that evening we had two concerts in the theatre. Not normal concerts; we had the 65 piece Hallé Orchestra along with tenors and sopranos and our

The Duchess of Cornwall returned to Queen Victoria in Liverpool

famous and friendly conductor Anthony Inglis. They were a triumph and saw standing ovations – especially as they performed the famous Liverpool Anthem 'You'll Never Walk Alone' – on Queen Victoria, on the Mersey in Liverpool, 170 years from when Samuel Cunard gave birth to this remarkable brand. If that was not enough we followed with fireworks and then to finish the evening off we had a Beatles Band to perform on board.

"So that was our day in Liverpool. It was just one day in the life of Cunard, just 55 minutes of our Godmother's time, just one day for the fine people of Liverpool but a very special day in the 62,000 days of our history."

ROYAL CELEBRATIONS

ANOTHER MOMENTOUS MILESTONE IN CUNARD LINE'S 171-YEAR HISTORY UNFOLDED AT SOUTHAMPTON ON MONDAY 11 OCTOBER 2010 – THE NAMING BY HM QUEEN ELIZABETH II OF THE LUXURIOUS NEW LINER BEARING HER NAME.

Buckingham Palace gave permission for Cunard Line to announce Her Majesty's participation in the ceremony a little over six weeks before it was to take place.

The news was widely expected although never taken for granted by senior officials at Cunard Line and its parent company Carnival UK.

With the all clear from the Palace, Cunard Line made the following announcement on 1 September 2010:

"Cunard Line is pleased to confirm that Her Majesty the Queen will name the company's new Queen Elizabeth, the third Cunard ship to bear the name, at a ceremony to take place in Southampton on Monday, 11 October 2010.

"The naming will be a milestone in British maritime history and will be a major event of worldwide interest.

"Peter Shanks, Cunard President and Managing Director, said: 'The naming of a Cunard Queen is a very special occasion and this will be an historic event in the true sense of the word. The Queen launched Cunard's Queen Elizabeth 2 in 1967 and named our current flagship, Queen Mary 2, in 2004. We are both honoured and proud that Her Majesty will name our new liner Queen Elizabeth.'"

Her Majesty was also present at the age of 12, at the launch of the first Queen Elizabeth on 27 September 1938, when she accompanied her mother, Queen Elizabeth, to Clydebank for the launch.

Cunard's Queen Elizabeth was due to set sail on her maiden voyage the day after her naming. The gala ceremony was to re-affirm Cunard Line's historic links with the Royal Family stretching back to 1934.

In that year Her Majesty Queen Mary, wife of King George V, launched Queen Mary – and in so doing became the first British Monarch ever to launch a merchant ship. His Majesty King George V accompanied his wife.

The late Queen Mother, as Her Majesty Queen Elizabeth, launched Queen Elizabeth in 1938. Princess Elizabeth and Princess Margaret accompanied their mother.

Her Majesty The Queen, as Princess Elizabeth, launched Caronia, the 'Green Goddess', in 1947. She was accompanied by HRH The Duke of Edinburgh.

HRH The Princess Margaret launched Carinthia in 1955.

Her Majesty The Queen launched Queen Elizabeth 2 in 1967. She was accompanied by

HRH The Duke of Edinburgh and HRH The Princess Margaret. Her Majesty The Queen named Queen Mary 2 in 2004; she was accompanied by HRH The Duke of Edinburgh. HRH The Duchess of Cornwall named Queen Victoria in Southampton in December 2007. She was accompanied by HRH The Prince of Wales.

A little less than three years later, the port of Southampton prepared to welcome another new Cunard Queen.

Following delivery from the Fincantieri shipyard at Monfalcone in Italy, and under the command of her new Master, Captain Chris Wells, Queen Elizabeth and her new crew made for their home port.

The ship arrived in Southampton Water for the first time on Friday, 8 October 2010 with thousands of well-wishers greeting the liner and her crew.

Queen Elizabeth berthed at the city's newest cruise facility, the striking Ocean Terminal.

Her Majesty the Queen during an earlier visit to QE2

The Queen meeting officers on board QE2

It is the city's fourth such facility capable of handling the complex logistics of disembarking as many as 3,000 guests and their luggage; replenishing on-board supplies from champagne and caviar, to bathrobes and bread and, a few hours later, welcoming as many as 3,000 new guests and their luggage.

For four days though, Queen Elizabeth was going nowhere.

A frantic programme of on-board visits for travel trade and media guests, together with other key suppliers and Carnival UK partners took place over the weekend – together with final preparations for the Royal Naming Ceremony. These included a rehearsal under conductor Anthony Inglis.

Passengers on board Hythe and Isle of Wight ferries crossing Southampton Water, could hear the Bournemouth Symphony Orchestra being put through its paces before its Royal appointment the following afternoon.

Ashore, security around the Terminal remained tight ahead of the arrival of the Royal party.

Naming day dawned bright under cloudless skies above Southampton – to the relief of those planning the largely outdoor event.

Ceremonies to mark the official naming of new liners entering service in the cruise industry have become a major part of establishing the profile of countless new vessels.

Lines with a fraction of the history and heritage of Cunard Line – and with none of the Line's association with the British Royal Family – rely on celebrity endorsement of their new ships, inviting artists, performers and sports stars to officiate at naming events.

As befits the operators of the most famous ocean liners in the world, things are done rather differently at a Cunard Royal Naming.

Cunard Line's 1,600 guests gathered inside the Ocean Terminal enjoying champagne

Her Majesty the Queen names the new Cunarder

Lesley Garrett performs at the launch of Queen Elizabeth

*Bournemouth
Symphony Orchestra
and Guardsmen
entertaining guests*

and canapés before making their way to a grandstand built specially on the quayside directly beneath the starboard side bridge wing and bow.

To their left, guests had a view of the Royal Platform and to the right, the huge stage constructed for the Bournemouth Symphony Orchestra and Bournemouth Symphony Chorus, together with soloists Lesley Garrett and Alexander Howard-Williams.

Between the Royal platform and the stage, in front of the huge grandstand, a large area of the quayside had been converted into a parade ground for massed marching bands from the Coldstream Guards and the Scots Guards. The vivid blue carpet beneath their parade-gloss shiny boots was emblazoned with a giant Cunard lion rampant emblem in starkly contrasting gold.

HM The Queen completed a tour of the ship before taking her place for the naming ceremony.

The Royal Tour was relayed via video link to the guests in the grandstand. On the bridge Captain Wells invited Her Majesty to sound the ship's whistle – the blast raising loud cheers from the guests and a smile from the Queen.

The Royal tour descended from the bridge and disembarked the ship. Moments later the Royal motorcade pulled into the dockside arena and Her Majesty took her place on the platform alongside Carnival Corporation & plc CEO

Micky Arison and Cunard Line President and Managing Director Peter Shanks.

He told guests: "I am delighted to welcome you to a truly historic occasion both for Cunard Line and for the whole of Great Britain- the naming of Queen Elizabeth.

"All of us at Cunard feel a great sense of pride at today's ceremony, this pride stems from the continuation of our distinguished heritage, and, of course, from the presence of Her Majesty the Queen."

The afternoon's formalities started with the National Anthem, followed by Jerusalem before words of welcome from Peter Shanks. Lesley Garrett then sang a specially arranged version of Amazing Grace followed by prayers of blessing by the Right Reverend Michael Scott-Joynt, Lord Bishop of Winchester.

At this point in proceedings, silence fell across the quayside as Captain Wells invited Her Majesty to perform the Naming of his new ship.

As the Queen uttered the words: "I name this ship Queen Elizabeth...", the fanfare trumpeters of the Irish Guards played the specially arranged Cunard Fanfare to loud cheers and applause.

Traditionally Cunard ships have been christened with wine rather than champagne, the only exceptions to this have been at the most recent naming of Queen Mary 2 and Queen Victoria where Veuve Clicquot Champagne was used in recognition of that brand's on board presence.

With no area designated as a Veuve Clicquot Champagne Bar on board Queen Elizabeth, naming ceremony traditions were retained and Her Majesty's words were celebrated by the smashing of a jeroboam of Cunard Graves, Baron Philippe de Rothschild, 2009.

Half a mile away in Southampton's Mayflower Park, further cheering broke out as spectators followed events live on a giant screen.

Moments later the Royal party took its leave.

Queen Elizabeth's naming had been a resounding success – marking the start of the ship's service as a Cunarder.

Maiden arrival –
Queen Elizabeth in
Southampton

CAPTAIN'S WELCOME

ONE OF QUEEN MARY 2'S LONGEST SERVING OFFICERS IS MASTER OF THE NEWEST CUNARDER IN THE FLEET.

Cunard Line announced the appointment of Queen Elizabeth's first Captain on 2 September 2009.

Captain Chris Wells joined Cunard as second officer on Queen Elizabeth 2 in 1992.

The 54-year-old Captain, who met his wife Hedda on QE2, was born and brought up in Bournemouth, and educated at Poole Grammar School.

His love of the sea developed when he learned to sail in Poole Harbour, and resulted in his commencing a four-year cadetship with Shell Tankers at Warsash College in 1974, qualifying as a second officer in 1978.

He obtained his Master's certificate in 1985.

Captain Wells served with Shell for 16 years, also finding time in 1986 to join the Royal Naval Reserve. He still undertakes two weeks' training with the RNR each year, and was promoted to the rank of Lieutenant Commander in 1994.

After joining Cunard and QE2, Captain Wells worked his way through the ranks to become staff captain. He later was seconded to the Queen Mary 2 New Build Team and spent 18 months at the St Nazaire shipyard in Brittany where the mighty transatlantic liner was built.

Having seen the ship develop from the beginning, and bringing her into service as Staff Captain, Captain Wells was extremely proud when appointed to the command of Queen Mary 2 last year.

Peter Shanks, President and Managing Director of Cunard Line said at the time of Captain Wells' appointment to Queen Elizabeth: "It is a well deserved honour for Captain Wells to be appointed Master of Queen Elizabeth. He is a fine leader for all of our colleagues working with him on Queen Elizabeth. His experience on both QE2 and Queen Mary 2 will ensure he continues the famous traditions of Cunard Line. Among these will be the maiden call of Queen Elizabeth to Liverpool. It promises to be another memorable day for the city and for Cunard Line."

Captain Wells names the day of the ship's Royal Naming as one of the proudest in his Cunard service.

Captain Wells lives in Barnham, West Sussex, with his wife and three children.

YOUNGEST FLEET AFLOAT

CUNARD LINERS MAY BELONG TO ONE OF THE OLDEST PASSENGER SHIPPING LINES IN HISTORY – BUT THEY ARE AMONGST THE MOST TECHNICALLY ADVANCED AND SOPHISTICATED AT SEA.

Queen Elizabeth and her near identical sister Queen Victoria are based on the Vista class of hull designed by the Italian naval architects and ship builders Fincantieri.

The design is a proven workhorse of the cruise industry in a similar way to that in which some of the Boeing Corporation's passenger aircraft have been universally taken into service by many airlines.

Cunard Line's parent company Carnival Corporation and plc uses this Vista class design across a number of its ocean going brands including Cunard Line, Holland America Line, Costa Crociere and P & O Cruises.

This has helped reduce design and build costs for successive orders and the ingenuity of the interior design teams working on each vessel for the individual lines, or Carnival brands, ensures a different "look & feel" inside each Vista class vessel.

QUEEN ELIZABETH'S TECHNICAL SPECIFICATION:

KEY DATES:

CONTRACT SIGNED:	OCTOBER 2007
KEEL LAYING:	2 JULY /JUNE 2009
FLOAT OUT:	5 JANUARY 2010
SEA TRIALS:	AUGUST AND SEPTEMBER 2010
NAMING CEREMONY:	11 OCTOBER 2010
MAIDEN VOYAGE:	12 OCTOBER 2010 - 13-NIGHT ATLANTIC ISLES VOYAGE

VITAL STATISTICS:

TONNAGES	GROSS: 90,900 GRT
LENGTHS	OVERALL: 964.5 FEET (294.0 METRES) BEAM: 106 FEET (32.25 METRES) BEAM AT BRIDGE WINGS: 36.8 METRES DRAFT: 26.2 FEET (8.0 METRES)
HEIGHTS	KEEL TO FUNNEL: 64.6 METRES (TO THE TOP OF THE FUNNEL LIGHT MAST)
ABOVE WATERLINE:	56.6 METRES

ITINERARIES:

	WORLD CRUISE
	LINER VOYAGES
	EXOTIC VOYAGES
	EUROPEAN VOYAGES FROM SOUTHAMPTON
	TRANSATLANTIC CROSSINGS

QUEEN ELIZABETH IS THE SECOND LARGEST CUNARDER EVER BUILT.

GENERAL:

BUILT BY	FINCANTIERI CANTIERI NAVALI SPA MONFALCONE SHIPYARD (NEAR TRIESTE).
PORT OF REGISTRY:	SOUTHAMPTON
SIGNAL LETTERS:	GBTT (THE SAME AS QE2)
SHIPYARD HULL NUMBER:	6187
CLASSIFICATION SOCIETY:	LLOYD'S REGISTER +100A1 PASSENGERS SHIP
GUEST CAPACITY:	LOWER BERTH 2,092 SPACE RATIO 44
NATIONALITY OF OFFICERS:	MAINLY BRITISH
NATIONALITY OF CREW:	INTERNATIONAL
DECKS:	TOTAL 16
	GUEST 12

MECHANICS:

DIESEL ENGINES:	SIX MAK M43C DIESEL ENGINES PODS: TWO ABB PODS
THRUSTERS:	THREE FINCANTIERI RIVA TRIGOSO THRUSTERS
SPEED:	NORMAL CRUISING SPEED: 21.7 KNOTS
	MAXIMUM SPEED: 23.7 KNOTS
STABILISERS:	A PAIR OF FINCANTIERI RIVA TRIGOSO
ANCHORS:	TWO ANCHORS (AND A SPARE)

THE TASTE OF SUCCESS

THE CULINARY EXPERIENCE AVAILABLE TO GUESTS TRAVELLING WITH CUNARD IS LEGENDARY.

The part played by food – and drink – in the Line's voyages around the world has come a long way since Sir Samuel Cunard's early days when a cow travelled on board ships, bearing his name to provide fresh milk.

Nowadays, service and the supply of fresh provisions are a little more sophisticated to say the least. Creating and maintaining mouth watering menus served to the highest standards of White Star Service have become a hallmark of Cunard Line.

As ships have grown in size, so too have passenger numbers – and the behind the scenes infrastructure required to meet growing expectations.

Twin brothers Nicholas and Mark Oldroyd, originally from East Yorkshire, each hold the position of Executive Chef with Cunard Line, Mark on board

Queen Mary 2 and Nicholas on Queen Elizabeth.

Nicholas explains how his main Galley serving the ship's two-deck Britannia Restaurant operates:

"The Galley has two main doors to maintain 'clean' and 'dirty' separation.

"All staff enter through the door leading to the 'dirty' section dropping off their dirty plates, linen etc

"They then pass by a dedicated hand washing machine where they wash their hands before moving into the 'clean' Galley environment.

"A team sorts all the returned glassware, crockery, cutlery and linen from every table and deals with the waste. With more than 800 guests in the Britannia, there could potentially be 20,000 plus items passing through this team's hands during any one meal period.

"We have large conveyor dishwashers where everything is washed with hot soapy water then rinsed, then blasted with ultra-hot water to kill any bacteria. The process has to be rapid. A domestic dishwasher at home may take an hour. Our system takes two minutes!

"The Galley has been carefully planned and laid out. The Beverage Station relies on huge supplies of fresh water – more than the ship can store in its tanks. So we rely on two huge salt water evaporators processing around 450 tonnes per day.

"The next important area of the Galley is the Garde Manager or Cold Larder. It's a busy area and produces all the cold appetizers, salads, cheese plates etc. It also produces up to 6,500 individually handmade cold hors d'oeuvres in any one voyage for all the receptions hosted by the Captain, as well as for serving in the bars and for guests in suite accommodation.

"Here the Sous Chef will produce a daily show plate of the dishes required and his team will set to work to produce the same dish hundreds of times over.

"These are placed on large racks and slide straight into large chiller cabinets until it is time to serve them. The same system operates in the Pastry area of the Galley. Every single dessert, petit four, or pastry item found anywhere on the ship is created here under the watchful eye of the Executive Pastry Chef who produces the same sort of show plate detailing that day's requirements for his team to produce."

Mark and his team cover a total of nine separate Galleys on board Queen Elizabeth and the logistics of keeping each supplied with the right ingredients at the right time are complex.

He explains: "We have a Provisions Team of ten people who take care of the loading of all the stores. They issue the required provisions for all Food & Beverage outlets twice daily.

"The storerooms on Queen Elizabeth consist of 17 huge refrigerators, freezers and dry stores for all items. The ship loads fresh stores – including milk, vegetables and fruits, fresh fish and seafood – approximately every seven days. Dry and frozen products are loaded approximately every 12 to 14 days depending on the ship's schedule.

"The Food & Beverage Department submits food requisitions up to three months in advance for longer voyages but typically every three to four weeks for shorter voyages."

Nicholas Oldroyd, Executive Chef on board the Queen Elizabeth

THE STATISTICS BEHIND SOME OF THE GALLEY TEAM'S MOUTH WATERING CREATIONS ARE THEMSELVES EYE WATERING! DURING AN AVERAGE 14 DAY VOYAGE THOSE ON BOARD QUEEN ELIZABETH WILL CONSUME:

- 70 tons of fruit and vegetables
- 18 tons of meat
- 12 tons of poultry
- 20 tons of seafood
- 30 tons of dairy products (excluding milk)
- 3 tons of sugar
- 67,850 pints of milk
- 4,666 dozen eggs
- 8 tons of flour

- 3 tons of rice
- 1,680 pizzas
- 11,200 scones
- 70,000 cups of tea
- 4,000 pints of beer
- 3,500 bottles of beer / cider
- 5,250 bottles of wine
- 530 bottles of champagne

THE TEAM WILL SERVE OVER 90,000 MEALS ON A 14 DAY VOYAGE AND CLEAN OVER A MILLION PIECES OF CHINA AND GLASS. ENOUGH WORK TO BUILD UP AN APPETITE!

PAINTING OF A QUEEN

Royal portrait artist Isobel Peachey

Cunard Line's history and heritage are second to none.

For more than 170 years the name has been synonymous with the finest traditions of ocean travel – in many cases traditions set down by Sir Samuel Cunard himself and maintained to this day.

One unique aspect of Cunard history is the Line's association with Royalty.

In line with the Cunard tradition of commissioning appropriate sculpture or portraits for display on board each ship named by a member of the Royal Family, the company commissioned an official portrait of The Queen for the new Queen Elizabeth.

This new official portrait was unveiled by the artist at a private event at the National Portrait Gallery in London.

The portrait, which shows The Queen in the Yellow Drawing Room at Buckingham Palace, was painted by 32-year-old Lancashire-born Isobel Peachey.

Although an accomplished award-winning portrait artist, she had never before been commissioned to paint a royal portrait.

She said: "At my interview with Cunard, I answered many questions about how I would approach an important commission – but it was only at the end of the interview that the subject was revealed as The Queen. This was both a shock and a marvellous surprise".

Cunard's President and Managing Director, Peter Shanks, said: "Apart from being impressed by the quality of Isobel's work, which we originally saw on display in the National Portrait Gallery, we were keen to offer the commission to a young artist who had never before had such an opportunity. Isobel is, in fact, the youngest female artist ever to paint the Monarch, and the quality of the finished work is such that our confidence has been greatly rewarded. It is a truly wonderful picture of Her Majesty. It is even more remarkable when you consider that, lacking a private studio, she executed this magnificent painting in her mum's attic!"

The portrait is a three-quarter length painting which shows The Queen dressed in blue and

wearing Queen Victoria's collet necklace and earrings, which she also wore for her Coronation in 1953.

The Queen saw the finished portrait for the first time on the day she named the liner in Southampton. The portrait is displayed in a prominent position in the ship's Grand Lobby.

Cunard Line also commissioned new works from renowned maritime artist Robert Lloyd.

The artist has a worldwide reputation for producing visually stunning and technically accurate paintings for the marine industry, private individuals and museum collections.

His critically-acclaimed portfolio includes a number of stunning commissions completed for Cunard Line.

His interest in the sea started during his childhood in Wirral. It is a painting of the former Cunard Line flagship Queen Elizabeth 2 that give the artist most satisfaction.

He explains: "The painting was entitled 'Coming Home' and showed her sailing up Southampton water on her final call before sailing off to Dubai. She is shown at a very impressive angle looking sleek and handsome. It was quite a large painting about 7ft wide by 4 ft deep. It was commissioned by Cunard to celebrate this most historic of Liners and was unveiled by Her Majesty the Queen on board in Southampton."

*Maritime artist
Robert Lloyd*

The painting was displayed on board the QE2 until she made the final call to Southampton – the arrival depicted in the painting. On his final farewell visit to the ship, HRH The Duke of Edinburgh presented the work to the City of Southampton. Robert's association with Cunard Line started after a meeting with Liverpool-born retired Commodore Ron Warwick.

"I was first introduced to Cunard by Commodore Ron Warwick, I had just completed a painting for him of the QE2. He was master at the time and he invited me onboard whilst the ship was in Southampton."

Since then he has completed more than a dozen paintings for Cunard.

"The first one completed was presented to Margaret Thatcher to commemorate the QE2's part in the Falklands War. I believe she has

Robert Lloyd's painting of three Cunard Queens hangs on Queen Elizabeth

this painting hung in her drawing room at home. I've also completed paintings of the Queen Mary 2 as well as a number of other paintings for various occasions."

Robert completed a number of paintings for the Queen Elizabeth.

"There are conventional paintings which feature historic Cunard Ships such as the original Queen Elizabeth as well as two very large paintings 16ft x 5ft. One depicts the QE2, QM2 and the Queen Victoria when they met in Southampton in 2008 and the other shows the Queen Elizabeth entering Sydney Harbour."

UNDER THE MAESTRO'S BATON

THE SPACE AND SPLENDOUR OF LIVERPOOL CATHEDRAL HAS PROVIDED A FITTING BACKDROP FOR A SERIES OF SPECTACULAR CUNARD LINE CONCERTS DURING LINER VISITS TO THE CITY.

In 2011 the tradition continues with a special performance for Cunard's guests on board Queen Elizabeth when the ship makes its maiden call at Cunard's spiritual home.

The Cathedral Concerts, together with the lavish Royal naming ceremonies for each of the Queens in the current Cunard fleet, have been led by renowned conductor Anthony Inglis.

He says: "I love the Liverpool events. Cunard may have left their Liverpool offices some years ago, but the company's heart lives on there. There's something very special, not just for the passengers on board the ships, but for

Above: The QE2 in the Mersey

the people and the Port of Liverpool to see a Cunard ship back in the Mersey. We always try and reflect that spirit in the concerts there."

The first Cunard concert at Liverpool Cathedral took place during the Queen Elizabeth 2's 40th anniversary voyage around the British Isles in 2007.

The most famous ocean liner in the world captured attention on the Mersey by sailing in to open the city's long-awaited cruise liner berth at Princes Parade (within a good stone's throw of the Cunard Building).

But the climax to the day of celebrations was

to be observed at Liverpool Cathedral, rather than on the banks of the Mersey.

It was a concert none who attended will ever forget – including Anthony Inglis.

He recalls: "One of the highlights for me was the very first one we did in the Cathedral celebrating 40 years of the QE2, when suddenly the huge great west doors were flung open and the Band of the Scots Guards marched in playing 'Sailing'.

"They then joined the orchestra and choir for a most moving rendition of 'Close of Day'. The whole place stood later, as they marched out just after the Last Post had been sounded. The next year, Simon Weston introduced the Welsh Guards! There have been so many wonderful highlights in a wonderful setting."

The conductor's connection with Cunard Line owes much to a friend in Los Angeles.

"It's an extraordinary story," he explains.

"I was chatting with an old girlfriend who is a senior producer for Fox TV and lives in Los Angeles. She mentioned she had seen in the American press that the (then) world's largest ship was being launched and she thought that surely they'd want some music for the occasion.

Cunard concert at Liverpool Cathedral

"Knowing my association with the sea, she suggested I write and offer my services."

He adds: "She knew that I'd been brought up during the 60s in Cowes on the Isle of Wight and had often seen the liners departing Southampton for some exotic destination.

"In fact my brother and I became very good at recognising the different sounds of the fog horns from ship to ship as they reached the old lightship at Calshot Spit and gave either one blast for turning right or two for left. It was huge excitement for us small boys if they only gave one blast, as in those days they used to dredge the channel between the mainland and the Island through Hurst Castle and past The Needles, and if the tide was right, we knew they were going the fast way, and we would race them along Gurnard Point. We loved those ships and during the holidays a liner leaving Southampton Water was a highlight for us."

Guardsmen on parade at Liverpool Cathedral

The conductor shared these childhood memories with Cunard Line:

"I wrote to them mentioning this and that I was now a reasonably well recognised musician, and I would love to take part in the Naming Ceremony for the first new Queen in a number of years. Something of my passion must have communicated itself in my letter. I think it says quite a lot for the family way of thinking in Cunard that they liked the story and they liked the link."

Even closer links between the Line and family exist.

He explains: "It wasn't until a lot later I mentioned I am descended from Robert Napier, the man to whom Sam Cunard turned to install engines into his first ships and the circle was completed! My great-great-great grandfather was David Napier, the engineer who founded the company that produced the famous Napier-

Railton racing cars and first aero engines. His first cousin was Robert."

Before he wrote his letter Anthony Inglis had no connection with Cunard Line.

"I had only gazed longingly from afar at these magical ships, each of whom I knew from watching on shore had a character all of its own," he explains. "I vividly remember the old Queen Elizabeth which was my favourite liner, though I thought the United States and France were both beautiful ships. I preferred the look of the Queen Elizabeth to the Queen Mary, but maybe that was because I knew she was the bigger ship! I also recall the first sailing out of Southampton Water of Queen Elizabeth 2; now that was some gorgeous lady! I never knew I would become so closely involved with the new Cunard era and with the ending of QE2's service as a Cunarder."

The ceremony during which HM Queen Elizabeth named Cunard Line's flagship Queen Mary 2 has a place in cruise industry history.

Music formed a very important part of the Royal programme as Anthony Inglis recalls.

"I don't think the cruise world had seen anything like the naming ceremony for Queen Mary 2. It blew everyone away as it was so unexpected. Lots of people remember the day!

"We have of course equalled it since, and big events which are spectacular have now become synonymous with Cunard, and I like to think no-one tries to do it like us, because no-one could! It is very definitely a team process, which involves everyone expressing ideas and thoughts," he explains.

"I just remember that it was all very rushed and because of that, it was probably all the better for it: nothing focuses the brain better than close deadlines.

"The actual go-ahead for the ceremony was made very close to the event and it was a time of mad ideas which somehow blossomed into reality. Christmas also came in the middle as the ceremony was at the beginning of January.

"The day itself I remember was dominated by the weather as there was a maximum wind speed above which the purpose built auditorium on the quayside in which we held the event was considered not to be safe for the audience.

"As the morning wore on, the wind gradually increased and we were getting seriously worried that we would have to cancel.

"However, providence was on our side, and at the scheduled start of the performance, the speed was within safe parameters and the show went on. I also particularly remember the Kabuki drop, where a curtain falls quickly, to reveal the Queen Mary 2 at the climax of Heather Small singing her song Proud. There was a gasp from the audience and then huge cheering."

Left: Conductor Anthony Inglis

Above: Fanfare for Cunard in Liverpool Cathedral
Below: Katherine Jenkins at a Cunard ceremony

have a good old British knees-up with a Last Night of The Proms type concert with a choir formed from the passengers on board. I have to say this trip is always keenly anticipated by the musicians. They get treated, as all passengers do, like royalty and get paid as well!"

History and heritage from an enormously important part of Cunard Line's enduring appeal to passengers.

"We try to reflect this in the music. For this year's inaugural Round Britain voyage of the Queen Elizabeth we will try and do exactly that, and you'll have to take the voyage to find out how! In the past, I have either discovered or been told about various pieces associated with Cunard. Such as The Queen of the Seas song written about the old Queen Mary or the Ballad of Q4 written about QE2.

"I have even discovered an old Victor Sylvester number called The Queen Elizabeth Waltz, though that was more about the monarch than the ship. However, I made a medley of these tunes and then played it on board the Queen Victoria in Liverpool."

Since writing his letter to Cunard Line, Anthony Inglis has worked and sailed regularly – an experience he always finds emotional.

"It is emotional. Only because I know my ancestor played such a large part in the beginning of the Line. The Cunard experience is of course unrivalled anywhere and people might say I'm biased, but I really do think the ships feel like a family. I guess it is all part of that White Star Service. When I sail on board, I often gaze out on my balcony at the passing sea and think my ancestor would be so proud to see the Line, of which he was such an integral part at the beginning, still powering through the seas, still visiting ports far and wide and still bringing a huge amount of pleasure to passengers all over the world."

As well as welcoming each of the current Cunard queens into service, the conductor played a pivotal role in events to mark QE2's departure.

"When we said Goodbye to QE2, we came up with one of the most moving moments of the concert: the movement from Faure's requiem while the Pennant was furled. With the naming ceremonies, these are usually decided by what works for which section. So we had Proud for the reveal of the Queen Mary 2 and Katherine Jenkins singing some Carmen for the moment the Queen Victoria was revealed. The secret is combining great music for the right moment; not always so easy. I remember I was asked by Carol Marlow (the Cunard Line President) to suggest some music for the QM2 that was contemporary and magic. I came up with Hedwig's Theme from Harry Potter! Absolutely perfect for the occasion."

Anthony Inglis takes his own orchestra annually across the Atlantic on board Queen Mary 2.

"We give 2 concerts during the voyage. One celebrates America and during the other we

Anthony Inglis conducts at the naming of Queen Mary 2

AROUND THE WORLD

CUNARD QUEENS DRAW LARGE CROWDS OF ONLOOKERS TO QUAYSIDES AND OTHER PORT VANTAGE POINTS ALL OVER THE WORLD – AND CROWDS AT THE LINE'S SPIRITUAL HOME OF LIVERPOOL ARE OFTEN AMONG THE LARGEST.

Even before September's arrivals in the Mersey of Queen Elizabeth and a week later Queen Mary 2, the most famous ocean liners in the world have made some very memorable, crowd-pulling appearances around the world in 2011.

The first was in New York – another city steeped in Cunard and transatlantic liner history.

On 14 January, Cunard Line's Three Queens made an historic rendezvous in New York Harbour during Queen Elizabeth's Maiden Call at Manhattan.

Thousands of New Yorkers turned out at vantage points from Battery Park at the tip of Manhattan Island to Hudson River Park to witness the spectacle, amidst fanfares and fireworks off the Statue of Liberty.

That meeting of the Queens marked only the second occasion that all three of the company's ships met together in the city. New York's first Cunard Royal Rendezvous took place in 2008 celebrating Queen Victoria's first arrival at the Big Apple.

The Line's President and Managing Director Peter Shanks commented: "Cunard Queens have always been regally greeted in our US home port, and we were thrilled that our newest Queen was met with an exquisite celebration. The city of New York is a core part of our legacy and a significant landmark for Cunard Line."

Main picture: Queen Mary 2 entering Sydney Harbour, Australia

Before the celebrations off Liberty Island, the President and MD joined Micky Arison CEO and Chairman of Cunard Line's parent company Carnival Corporation & plc and Cunard Line Commodore Bernard Warner at the New York Stock Exchange where the ship's bell from the original Queen Elizabeth was rung to mark the close of the day's trading.

Later that evening the Empire State Building was bathed in Cunard red to mark the special occasion.

A little over a month later the focus switched to another of the world's most famous harbours – Sydney.

Queen Elizabeth arrived there for the first time following her larger sister, Queen Mary 2, in another historic meeting of the Cunard Queens. That visit marked the first time two Cunard liners had ever arrived together in Sydney Harbour.

It also prompted memories for some of an earlier meeting when the original Queen Mary and Queen Elizabeth – both then World War II troop ships – passed each other at Sydney Heads on 9 April 1941.

Queen Elizabeth met Queen Mary 2 outside Sydney Heads before 5.30am before following her sister into the Harbour and berthing at the Overseas Passenger Terminal at around 7am. Both ships were midway through their world voyages, Queen Elizabeth having sailed from New Zealand while Queen Mary 2 arrived from Adelaide.

In March, still on her Maiden World Voyage, Queen Elizabeth arrived in Dubai for another poignant rendezvous with the ship that became the most famous Cunarder of all time – Queen Elizabeth 2

The iconic liner was sold to a Middle Eastern Consortium and left Cunard service in November 2008 after sailing to Dubai where it was intended to convert her into a static hotel. The planned conversion has been delayed and her immediate future remains uncertain.

QE2 and Queen Victoria in Sydney

QE2 and Queen Elizabeth in Dubai

FESTIVAL IS BACK
WITH A BANG

*Queen Elizabeth and Queen Mary 2 will join a firework
spectacular as part of the 2011 Mersey River Festival*

Tall Ships moored at the Albert Dock in Liverpool to a stunning back drop of the city

Cunard liners are set to take pride of place in the 2011 Mersey River Festival. The week long extravaganza has been specially planned around the visits to Liverpool of Queen Elizabeth and Queen Mary 2 in September. Queen Elizabeth's maiden call to Liverpool on 8 September will mark the official start of the Festival – the final part of the 2011 'On the Waterfront' series of free events staged by Liverpool City Council and its partners.

Queen Mary 2's second call to the Mersey, a week later on 15 September, will conclude the seven-day event. Both Cunarders will spend a full day berthed at the City of Liverpool Cruise Terminal during their respective round Britain voyages.

It is the first time Queen Elizabeth has sailed around the British Isles. She is scheduled to depart her home port of Southampton on the afternoon of 2 September, bound for South Queensferry on the Firth of Forth.

The following day she will call at Invergordon, north east Scotland, before a day at sea navigating her way to Greenock on the River Clyde near Glasgow. That day will be spent alongside the town with so many proud Cunard connections.

In the evening, the newest Cunarder will set a course for the Mersey, arriving the following morning when she is due alongside at 8am, to mark her maiden visit to Cunard Line's spiritual home and the start of the River Festival.

Civic dignitaries will join her Master, officers and some crew members at Liverpool Cathedral, for a special commemorative concert in the afternoon.

Queen Elizabeth will depart at 10pm after a firework display off Pier Head. The ship will head for Dublin with further calls at Cobh and St Peter Port, Guernsey, before her return to Southampton on 12 September.

Queen Mary 2's second cruise around the British Isles starts in the same port on the same day.

The flagship of the Cunard fleet will depart for Cherbourg before heading for Cobh, then Liverpool, arriving alongside at 12:15pm on Thursday, 15 September.

The mighty transatlantic liner will depart following fireworks at the Pier Head at 10pm, bound for Greenock, South Queensferry and Southampton. Her passage down the Mersey that evening will mark the finale of the 2011 River Festival.

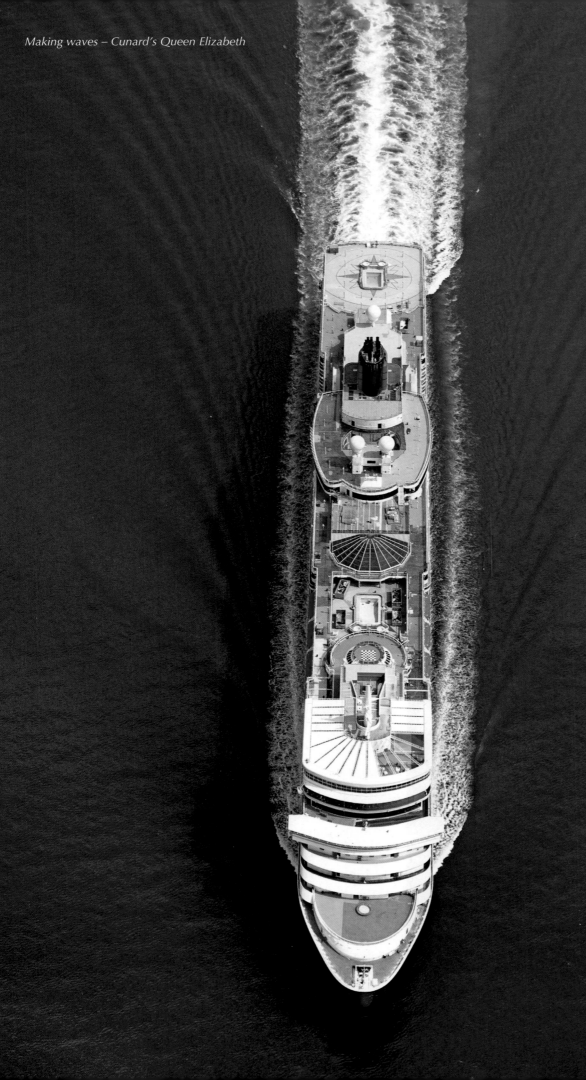

Making waves – Cunard's Queen Elizabeth